A BRIEF HISTORY

OF THE

UNIVERSALIST CHURCH

FOR YOUNG PEOPLE

BY

L. B. FISHER, D.D.

Fredonia Books
Amsterdam, The Netherlands

A Brief History of the Universalist Church for Young People

by
L. B. Fisher

ISBN: 1-4101-0108-8

Copyright © 2002 by Fredonia Books

Fredonia Books
Amsterdam, The Netherlands
http://www.fredoniabooks.com

All rights reserved, including the right to reproduce this book, or portions thereof, in any form.

In order to make original editions of historical works available to scholars at an economical price, this facsimile of the original edition is reproduced from the best available copy and has been digitally enhanced to improve legibility, but the text remains unaltered to retain historical authenticity.

DEDICATION.

To the Young People's Christian Union of the Universalist Church, under whose direction the author has compiled this volume, he dedicates his work. May this little volume be useful in building up the Kingdom of Christ on earth, and especially in aiding our young people in their efforts to make a Universalist Church which shall build its full share of that kingdom.

PREFACE.

It is believed that there is a place in the world for a history of our Church which is compiled especially for the new generation of young people, who may not have time to read the larger volumes written by Dr. Eddy and others. It is hoped that such a brief and condensed work may fill a place in our Sunday-schools and young people's meetings as a text-book. The young generation must be kept in living touch with the great work wrought by the Fathers. The Y.P.C.U. expects that this small volume may awaken a desire in many minds to read the larger volumes, and so to create a body of Universalists who have intelligent historical perspective. The coming Church will enter on its policies wisely and push them effectively when it does these things in the light of all our history. We want to know where our roots are, so we may wisely shape the plant that we expect to grow from those roots. This book is prepared out of a very busy life, and it is hoped that its imperfections will set some one to the task of making a much better one later. The author makes grateful acknowledgment of assistance from many friends.

L. B. FISHER.

CANTON THEOLOGICAL SCHOOL.

CONTENTS.

CHAPTER		PAGE
	Introduction	9
I.	The History of Ancient Universalism	15
II.	Universalism in America before John Murray	20
III.	John Murray	24
IV.	The Compeers of John Murray	33
V.	The Theology of John Murray	41
VI.	Hosea Ballou	48
VII.	The Theology of Hosea Ballou	56
VIII.	The Restoration Controversy	64
IX.	Some Other Leaders	71
X.	Universalist Societies, Parishes and Churches	77
XI.	Associations and Conventions	86
XII.	Universalist Creeds	100
XIII.	Universalists and Missionary Work	111
XIV.	Sunday-schools and Children	125
XV.	The Young People's Christian Union	138
XVI.	The Universalist Church and Education	155
XVII.	The Women of the Universalist Church	167
XVIII.	The Universalist Press	179
XIX.	Hymn Books and Liturgies	189
XX.	The Universalist Church of To-day	199

INTRODUCTION.

A HISTORY of Universalism may mean either of two things. It may mean an account of the rise and growth of the Universalist ideas, or it may mean the story of the organizing of the men and women who hold these ideas into what we to-day call the Universalist Church.

Men held Universalist ideas for a long time before there was any organized Universalist Church. Many to-day hold Universalist ideas who are not in the Universalist Church.

In the first chapter of this book something will be said of those who held the Universalist ideas but who never organized any denomination with that name. The other chapters will attempt to tell the story of the heroic endeavors of those who rejoiced to hold our ideas, but who, desiring that these ideas might prevail, strove to gather in one visible company all who held them. Before we come to our history, let us be sure that we understand what the Universalist ideas are. The distinctive Universalist idea is, that sometime, somewhere, — we set no date nor place, — every person will try to know God's will and obey it. In common phrase, it is that all will finally be saved; and this common phrase is true if only we attach the true meaning to the word "saved." One is saved when he can truly say with his Master, "It is my meat to do the will of him who sent me."

Universal means all, and we call ourselves Universalists because we believe that all will finally obey God. This will be Universal Salvation. We are Universalists because we believe in the Universals. We believe in the Universal Fatherhood of God; the Universal Brotherhood of Man; the coming Universal rule of Christ; the Universal triumph of God over evil. Universalist is a great name. Dr. Ryder said, "It is the only denominational name that stands for any leading quality of the divine government: it is the only denominational name that indicates what the results of the divine government will be."

When Mrs. Browning first heard this word as the name of a sect of Christians, she paused, repeated it reflectively, saying, "Universalist; what a beautiful name!" Let every one who bears this beautiful name be proud of it and strive to honor it.

Another thing to do here in this introduction to our little book, is to name the sources from which we get our facts, so that we will not need to fill our pages with repeated references to the

Introduction. 11

same books. We name these sources of our history for another reason.

It is hoped that many of our young people will resolve to know more of our history than they can learn from this little volume, and that they will have in their own libraries at least a few of the books referred to here. Those who know our history best will get the most personal help from their faith and be the best workers for its extension.

Our Publishing House is in Boston, at 30 West Street, and on request, will gladly tell you all about the books named here and many others. Many of the facts in this manual come from the files of our Church papers, which are kept in the libraries of our seminaries, and which also ought to be preserved in every Sunday-school library, together with all other books and periodicals relating to our faith.

Every young Universalist ought to visit the rooms of the Universalist Historical Society at Tufts College. This Society was formed by the General Convention in 1834, for the collection of facts, books, and papers pertaining to the history and condition of Universalism. The Society is incorporated under the laws of Massachusetts. It has a library of about five thousand volumes, beside important manuscripts and papers. Rev. Richard Eddy, D.D., is President of this Society; and no Universalist should ever allow any book or tract, that may have historical value, to be destroyed, without first corresponding with Dr. Eddy as to its usefulness.

Since 1836 a Universalist Register has been published annually, and these are full of most important and interesting figures and facts for us. The published minutes of the General Convention and the Annual Reports of the Board of Trustees of that body furnish constant historical data. For the history of ancient Universalism we have the works of Hosea Ballou 2d, and the volume on Retribution by Rev. Edward Beecher, D.D., and several valuable works by Rev. J. W. Hanson, D.D.

For the modern history of Universalism the reader will enjoy the books of Thomas Whittemore, and "Fifty Notable Years" by John G. Adams, and "A Century of Universalism" by Rev. Abel C. Thomas, D.D. Later, fuller, and better than all these, however, and containing the pith of them all and more, are Rev. Richard Eddy's two noble volumes on "The History of Universalism," covering the ground from 1636 to 1886. These are our standard volumes. Dr. Eddy also wrote the history of Universalism for the "American Church History Series," his chapters being in volume ten. The book entitled "Centennial of the Universalist Profession of Faith" contains the papers and addresses delivered at the Centennial meeting held at Winchester, N.H., in 1903. Then there are the interesting and inspiring biographies of our great leaders, which make as fine records of missionary zeal as the world can show.

Our young people will be charmed and thrilled by these biographies if they will read them. Get the lives of John Murray, Hosea Ballou, Dr. Ballou, W. S. Balch, E. H. Chapin, J. H. Chapin, Dr. Ryder, Dr. Miner, Dr. Sawyer, and Caroline Sawyer, and live awhile with these strong, clear souls. Then there are hosts of faithful prophets and apostles of the living God, preachers of the everlasting Gospel, of whom no full biography has ever been written. Not that they were not worthy, but no one has undertaken the task. From various scattered sources we gather brief fragments, how often too brief, of records and personal memories of noble men and women whose names are written in the Book of Life. O young Universalists, you are children of a sturdy stock, heirs of brave men and women, with clear brains and strong hearts, and you must live well if you would be worthy of your inheritance.

Unless we do better than our fathers and mothers did, we do not do as well.

A BRIEF HISTORY
OF THE
UNIVERSALIST CHURCH.

CHAPTER I.

THE HISTORY OF ANCIENT UNIVERSALISM.

This chapter tells of some who lived before the year 500 of our era, who held Universalist ideas, but who never organized themselves into a Church with our name. If we have had an idea that Universalism is something new, we shall be pleasantly surprised to learn how old it really is. Our organized denomination is only a few decades old, but men have nourished our beautiful faith for many centuries. Let us begin with the Bible. It is assumed, as it is impossible to attempt detailed proof here, that the Bible is a Universalist book. All our great Church Fathers built their doctrines on Scripture. Ballou and his contemporaries were pioneers in rational biblical interpretation, and while more is known of the Book to-day than they could have known, yet it is amazing to note in how many particulars their work stands. Almost daily do we hear announced with great flourish of trumpets, as new discoveries, interpretations of Scripture that Hosea Ballou made common currency for Universalists long ago. The older insistence on isolated texts has passed, and the theories of inspiration and of revelation have received some new statement, but in many ways the Bible work of our Fathers stands to-day. When we say that the Bible is a Universalist book, we mean that Universalism is the logic of the Bible. The Bible shows "a God absolutely on the side of mankind." It shows that "the movement of the whole moral power of the universe is toward a racial redemption," and that "God will have all men to be saved." If God succeeds, then Universalism is the result, and the Bible reveals a successful God.

The best work our Fathers did was to show that texts and words which were being used to prove that some souls were hopelessly lost, did not prove any such doctrine. In doing that work they placed the whole Christian world under a debt of gratitude, — a debt which that world is very slow in acknowledging. The Bible, in the sweep of a few mighty texts, still more in the logic of all its teachings, is a Universalist book. We delight to find our Universalist ideas in some great positive assertions; and still more clearly to find them as the only rational conclusions from the premises of the attributes of God, the nature of the soul, and the organic solidarity of the human race. These premises and conclusions are the word of God in the Book; they are also the universal word of God in instinct, reason, faith, and science.

After the Bible writers, we have many books written by men known as the Apostolic Fathers and the Ante-Nicene Fathers. From these books we learn that the young Church was mainly occupied in shaping the doctrines of Christianity, and defending it against attacks. On the question of final destiny the Church made no official utterance for more than five hundred years. Some teachers held to endless punishment, some to annihilation of the wicked, and some to universal salvation, and one of these opinions appears to have been as orthodox as another. One of these Fathers who held the Universalist idea was Clement Alexandrinus, who taught about 190-196 A.D. Here is one of Clement's lessons on Universalism.

"How is he a Saviour and Lord unless he is the Saviour and Lord of all? He is certainly the Saviour of those who have believed; and of those who have not believed he is the Lord, until by being brought to confess him, they shall receive the proper and well-adapted blessing for themselves." "The Lord is the propitiation, not only for our sins, that is for the faithful, but also for the whole world; therefore he indeed saves all; but converts some by punishments, and others by gaining their free will; so that he has the high honor, that to him every knee shall bow, of things in heaven, on earth, and under the earth; that is of angels, men, and the souls of those who died before his advent."

One of Clement's pupils was Origen, who lived from 185 to 253 A.D. Origen is the greatest name in the early Church after Paul, and Origen was a Universalist. Edward Beecher says, "Two great facts stand out on the pages of ecclesiastical history: One that the first system of Christian theology was composed and issued by Origen in the year 230 after Christ, of which a fundamental essential element was the doctrine of the Universal restoration of all fallen beings to their original holiness, and union with God. The second is, that after the lapse of a little more than three centuries, in the year 544 this doctrine was for the first time condemned and anathematized as heretical. This was done, not in a general council, but in a local council called by order of Justinian."

Another great man for us to remember as a Universalist is Theodore of Mopsuestia. He held "that sin is an unavoidable part of the development and education of man; that some carry it to a greater extent than others, but that God will finally overrule it for their final establishment in good."

During these centuries there were six Theological Schools in the Christian Church. Four of these schools taught the Universalist idea of destiny, one taught annihilation of the wicked, and one taught endless misery.

There are many other names that we ought to remember. Dean Farrar says that every scholar admits that Basil and Gregory taught the final restoration of all human souls. Thus we see that Universalism in the early Church was not hidden nor obscure, but was openly held by the greatest teachers and taught in the best schools.

As we have seen, a local council in 544 condemned Universalism as heresy, and history for the next thousand years is history of the Dark Ages. The Church passed from the shaping thought of these teachers of the Greek spirit, and came under the influence of the hard, mechanical Roman temper. God was simply an almighty Cæsar, ruling this world from his throne in the sky, sending his rebellious subjects to an awful, endless prison, out of sight and out of mind forever. Tertullian, Augustine, Calvin, Milton, and Dante ruled the Church, and Jesus and the Gospels were permitted to recede. If, then, any young Universalist is told that his doctrines are new, let him steadily assert that the doctrine of the final salvation of all souls was the prevailing opinion of the Christian Church for the first six centuries of her history.[1]

[1] Dr. Hanson's book, "Universalism in the First Five Hundred Years of the Christian Church," is filled with interesting facts for any reader who desires to pursue this study further See also "Ancient History of Universalism," by Hosea Ballou 2d, D D.; and "The Scriptural Doctrine of Retribution," by Edward Beecher, D.D.

CHAPTER II.

UNIVERSALISM IN AMERICA BEFORE JOHN MURRAY.

We pass from the sixth to the eighteenth century, and from the Old World to America. Many can be named in this gap who were Universalists, silently nourishing the great faith which the world seems to have forgotten. Dr. Whittemore found enough Universalism in Europe during this period to fill a volume published in its final form in 1860. But none of these whom we have found thus far holding our ideas had made any attempt to organize a Universalist Church. Whatever has been done to make our scattered believers into a Church has been done in America. Even here we do not at any fixed date pass from unorganized to organized Universalism. We do not leap into Church life, we slowly grow. As we shall see, our people have always been as they are now, reluctant to become communicants in the Church, and indifferent to appeals to place themselves where they count the most for effective organization. This tendency to stand aloof and alone, or not to see beyond the local parish, appears in all our history, and is the sufficient answer to the question as to why we are a small body. We are too much a lot of independent scattered individuals, or of local parish groups with no splendid "ésprit de corps." Let every young Universalist see this weakness that cripples us, and strive to cure it. Let us be a Church, and not a "go-as-you-please" saunter.

John Murray is the father of our organized Church, but a word is to be said of what he found in America on his arrival here in 1770. Dr. Eddy names five sources of Universalism existing in our country before this date. He names as these sources the Mystics, the Dunkers, the Moravians, the Episcopalians, and the Congregationalists, citing from all these sects the names of many who held the Universalist ideas. This prevalence of the Universalist idea is in part the explanation of the fact that Murray found so many churches open to him and that so many invitations to preach were sent to him. Murray found first, Thomas Potter, who all alone had reached the Universalist conclusion, and erected a meeting-house, and was waiting in confidence for the Lord to send him a preacher.

Dr. George de Benneville, 1703–1793, is a name to be kept in loving remembrance. This man was cast out of the Church of England for preaching the restoration of all souls. Obedient to the Divine Voice, he bore his message to France. For preaching this gospel there, he was arrested in Calais, and imprisoned, and warned that his life would be the forfeit if he preached again. Preach he did, however, to great crowds, and was again arrested, with a friend named Durant. This friend was hanged, meeting his death with serenity and courage. De Benneville was sentenced to be beheaded, and his hands were already bound, when a reprieve arrived. Then for eighteen years he preached in Germany, where he had that remarkable trance vision in which as a mystic De Benneville believed, but which he reluctantly told of for fear of the misinterpretation of visionless people. He was sick, and thinking him dead his friends prepared his body for burial. Reviving, he told how his spirit had joined the heavenly host beyond, and had heard them singing, "An eternal restoration, an everlasting restitution of all things." This brave man came to Pennsylvania in 1741. He was a physician and a preacher. At Oley, where De Benneville married, he built a house with a hall seating fifty people, in which he often preached. He caused Paul Siegvolk's book, "The Everlasting Gospel," to be translated, printed, and widely circulated. This book was the instrument of leading many into the light of Universalism.

Here is the first preacher, the first chapel, and the first published book of our faith in America. In 1790 De Benneville wrote his daughter, "In my old age, since I am eighty years old, my mind is still set to preach the Gospel." A noble man to remember is George de Benneville. Our church is greatly indebted to Rev. James Shrigley, one of our living saints, for our knowledge of this first American preacher of Universalism.

Some four years before Murray saw the place, there was a little company of Universalists in Gloucester, Mass. About 1770 a Mr. Gregory had brought there a copy of a book by James Relly, known as "Union," which had been read, and so could not be forgotten, and they were waiting for a preacher, as was Potter. "Relly's Union" was another great Universalist book in its day. This appears to be all the known Universalism in America before John Murray, but we may fairly suppose that many hearts were ready for the word, and waiting for the prophet.

CHAPTER III.

JOHN MURRAY.

JOHN MURRAY is the father of our organized Church. He was born in Alton, England, in 1741. We see him there in his early manhood a fervent preacher of Calvinism. There was in London at this time a Universalist preacher named James Relly; and a young woman of Whitefield's congregation had become interested in his message, and John Murray was sent to show her the dreadful danger she was in, and to bring her back to the true fold. This young woman appears to have been a person of parts; and she asked John some questions which had their way in him, until he went to hear Relly preach, and became a Universalist himself.

While these theological changes were working so intensely in Murray's sensitive mind, his wife died. The expenses of her sickness left Murray in debt; and his creditors, glad to have a chance to punish him for his heresy, had him imprisoned for this debt. Soon released, he engaged in business until all debts were paid. Persecuted by his former religious associates, deserted by all his friends save Mr. Relly, lonely and sad-hearted, he resolved to bury himself in America, and never preach again.

So in 1770, being twenty-nine years old, our Jonah set sail in the brig "Hand in Hand," to hide himself and his message in the wilderness. By mistake the brig got into Cranberry Inlet on the New Jersey coast, and there ran aground. To lighten and release her, part of her cargo was transferred to a smaller vessel, which was left in Murray's charge with instructions to bring it to New York at the earliest moment possible.

Delayed by contrary winds, Murray went ashore for food, and met Thomas Potter, who generously supplied his needs, and insisted that after providing for his men, he return and be his guest that night. "For," said Potter to the surprised supercargo, "I have been expecting you for a long time." So the Lord's prophet finds his waiting servant. Potter by his fireside that night told Murray his life's story. He told how he could neither read nor write, but he could think, and alone with God's Spirit he had thought his way into the Universalist idea; and how, derided by his neighbors, he had all alone built a church, and had been waiting all those years for God to send him a preacher. He declared that as Murray entered his yard that afternoon, the Voice said, "Potter, this man is your preacher."

Murray protested, and insisted that he must depart with the first fair wind, but Potter steadily maintained that winds nor tides would never serve until his preacher spoke his word. Murray held out against all entreaty until Saturday afternoon, and then yielded to the power not himself; and Potter's men spread the word that the long-looked-for preacher had appeared, and that he would preach the next day. So the sloop lay windbound while its awestruck master preached in Thomas Potter's meeting-house. On this historic spot, so sacred to all true Universalists, now stands the beautiful Potter Memorial Church, and here each returning summer, under the auspices of the "Murray Grove Association," a company gathers, and enjoys delightful days at this shrine.

This "Murray Grove Association" was organized on Aug. 24, 1866, for the purpose of "providing means, adopting and executing measures, for the preservation of memorials and property endeared to Universalists at Good Luck, N.J., and for holding yearly meetings thereat during each summer in the interests of the Church at large." The Association is a legally incorporated body, and owns the Murray Grove House and furniture, subject, at present writing, to some debt, which every Universalist might well help to remove. Rev. T. B. Payne is President and Rev. V. E. Tomlinson

Vice-President of the Association. Rev. E. G. Mason, and Mr. John C. Dessalet of Philadelphia, and Mr. James B. McNeal of Baltimore, deserve the gratitude of all our people for the lively interest they have taken in all the good works of this Association.

In the summer of 1902 a memorial boulder was set up and dedicated at Good Luck, with this inscription upon it: —

> "Near this spot first met Thomas Potter the Prophet and John Murray the Apostle of Universalism. The following Sunday, Sept. 30, 1770, in Potter's Meeting-House, Murray first preached in America. The wilderness and the solitary place were glad for them."

Dr. Atwood dedicated and consecrated this memorial, and Mr. Dessalet sprinkled it with water that he had brought from the Jordan.

Murray often returned to this spot, and ardently desired that it might be his home; but as his duties multiplied, his visits, first frequent, grew more and more rare; and in 1782 he came and found the master dead, and so never came again. Potter willed his meeting-house and an acre of land about it to Murray, and his large estate to his wife. He had no child to carry out his wishes, and unscrupulous administrators alienated both the church and the estate. The good wife died in the poorhouse, and the Methodists now hold the old meeting-house. Let us gratefully remember Thomas Potter:

> "For a dreamer lives forever,
> But a toiler dies in a day."

Murray got his sloop to New York in due season, and there his career as a sailor abruptly ended, and he came to his own proper office again. Before he had been in New York a day, he was invited to preach in a Baptist church. Calls to preach came from every side, and the preacher ran away no more. The wilderness in which he thought to hide became vocal with calls to service, and the preacher went hither and thither to respond. He came greatly to enjoy the itinerant life; and being a ready speaker, full of anecdote and illustration, a man of impressive presence and remarkable conversational powers, he was everywhere popular, and so preached everywhere from Maryland to New Hampshire.

In addition to his almost daily preaching, Murray attended to the publication of a small pamphlet, written by his London teacher, Relly, entitled, "A Short Specimen of Apostolic Preaching." Within ten years from Mr. Murray's coming, two other volumes of Mr. Relly's books were issued. One of these was a volume of "Hymns, Poems and Spiritual Songs," and the other was "Union," referred to later in this book. Mr. Murray sold his horse to pay the expenses of the first publication, but kind friends in Newport, R.I., soon after made good this loss.

Murray had not long been in America before his theology became an object of suspicion, and he himself was attacked by many a sharp tongue and envenomed pen. Some enemy, through the press, called him a "Rellyan." The little group at Gloucester, made up of those who had seen Relly's book, already spoken of, heard of this attack on Mr. Murray, and, being naturally interested, they sent for the "Rellyan" to come and visit them.

So in 1774 Murray came to Gloucester, and for twenty years that town was his home as much as such a wanderer can be said to have had a home. Murray held his first meeting in Gloucester at the house of Mr. Winthrop Sargent, and there met Mr. Sargent's widowed daughter, who in due time became Mrs. Judith Murray. Mrs. Murray was a woman of marked personal beauty, with a quick and vigorous intellect, and was always an intensely loving and loyal wife, very jealous for her husband's honor. She outlived Mr. Murray for some years, and published the Autobiography he had been preparing for some time, herself adding some closing chapters to the volume.

John Murray's life in Gloucester had its sorrows as well as its joys. He faced much sectarian bigotry, and had many relentless enemies; and so, while he was by all his nature a man of peace, he was forced to keep his armor on and his sword unsheathed continually nearly all his life. But he also had many loving and influential friends. Among the latter were Generals Washington and Greene. They chose Murray chaplain of a regiment in spite of vigorous protest of the other chaplains that a heretic should not be in such an office. He filled this office for eight months, and then was forced to resign by sickness. That winter there was severe suffering in Gloucester, as her business had been ruined by the war. Murray went among his army friends, and raised a large sum of money to relieve the needs of his destitute neighbors, Washington himself signing ten pounds. For this service the town gave Mr. Murray a vote of thanks. This was in 1776; and before that year ended, a mob collected round the house of the man who had fed them, determined to ride him out of town. He was several times warned to leave Gloucester at once, and threatened with violence if he stayed. Mr. Murray knew even what it meant to be stoned in the streets, to such length did zeal against heretics madden the people. At one formal town-meeting, the question whether Mr. Murray should leave town was voted upon, and the vote stood fifty-four to eight in favor of his going at once. Still he quietly stayed, and faithfully did his work. He was told that he was a "false teacher," a "spy," a "Romanist in disguise;" and one good man up in Portsmouth, a minister too, said that Mr. Murray had at one time privately confessed to him that he did not believe Universalism at all. So Mr. Murray took a trip to Portsmouth, to try to induce this teacher of piety to tell the truth, but returned unsuccessful.

At this time in New England, the parish was the town; and every citizen, regardless of his opinions, was taxed to support the minister chosen by the majority. So even after Mr. Murray's congregation had withdrawn, and built a meeting-house of their own, the assessors of the First Parish tried to force them to pay taxes to support that body. In 1782 they seized and sold at auction goods of Universalists to enforce payment of this tax. This kept Mr. Murray and his parish in a distasteful and expensive lawsuit, which was not settled until 1786. These gentlefolk at one time tried to make Mr. Murray leave town because he was a "vagrant," but a friend gave him a deed of some property, and he stayed a freeholder. At last they declared that he was not an ordained clergyman; and so, with all due regard for legal detail, he was ordained again.

After a time Mr. Murray began to preach half the Sundays in Boston. At one of his first sermons there, some one threw a heavy stone at him in the desk. Quietly he held the missile in his hand, and said that while as an argument it was solid and weighty, yet it was neither scriptural nor convincing. In 1793 Mr. Murray moved to Boston, and, although often urged to do so, he never changed residence again. Here he had a large and influential church, a comfortable estate, a loving wife and daughter, and, if his enemies increased, his friends did much more abound.

He preached as long as strength permitted, and in 1815 died, as much as a good man can die. His body was first placed in the Sargent family tomb; but in 1837 our people bought a lot in Mount Auburn, and erected a monument, and there lies the dust of John Murray.

CHAPTER IV.

THE COMPEERS OF JOHN MURRAY.

In this chapter let us study some of those who labored beside John Murray in building the organized Universalist Church.

We will fix our attention on the year 1785. This year an association met at Oxford, which was about the first gathering of Universalists of different parishes that had been attempted. Murray was now about forty-five years of age, and had been fifteen years in America. As far as we know, there were nine laymen, representing five parishes, and four ministers present. We know, however, of twelve Universalist ministers beside Mr. Murray who were preaching at this time. Here let us note the names of the twelve apostles of our faith in 1785.

The names are David Evans, Noah Murray, Zephaniah Lathe, Thomas Barns, Clement Sumner, Moses Winchester, Elhanan Winchester, Adams Streeter, Noah Parker, Caleb Rich, Matthew Wright, and George de Benneville. What stirring stories of battles for their faith these twelve could tell, and how helpful and inspiring it would be to listen to them! Some of them we must know about, because they are so prominent in our history.

Caleb Rich was born in Sutton, Mass., in 1750. He was of a sensitive spirit, and the attempt to believe the accepted doctrine of his day about the fate of the lost was unspeakable torment to him. This unfortunate struggle embittered all his early years. If he tried to pray, he was haunted with the thought that it was all a selfish desire to escape hell. He was one of the young men who see visions, and the old men who dream dreams. He was led along his way by these dreams to begin a study of the Bible for himself. He came to think that all the children of Adam and Eve before the fall died in sin when their parents sinned, and would be restored and made alive in Christ, while all born to our first parents after the fall would cease to exist at the death of the body. Caleb and his brother Nathaniel, and a Joseph Goodell, held this idea, and so could not belong to the Baptists, and therefore the three formed a society of their own. These three devout souls remind us of the early Methodists in their intense piety.

After a time Caleb came to see that even the children of Eve after the fall were not out of God's reach. In April, 1778, Caleb the dreamer saw the grandest vision of all, and henceforth he knew that God was the loving, saving Father of even the children born after the fall. Now he had a Gospel and felt a call to preach, and forthwith began his work.

Mr. Rich had heard of John Murray, but it was a long way in those days from New Hampshire to Gloucester, and they had not met perhaps until this Oxford Association. About 1781 a union meeting of three New Hampshire parishes ordained Mr. Rich, which ordination his enemies questioned, but the courts ratified. So this good man, with his clear spirit that saw what most men cannot, preached for more than thirty years with no more torment, but ever deepening love and longing for all the children of God. Those who knew him loved him as a devout Catholic loves a saint, and they spoke of him as "Father Rich."

Another minister at this Oxford meeting in 1785 was Adams Streeter. He came to us from the Baptists about 1778. His brother Zebulon said once, "I would willingly part with all my earthly possessions if it would make me able to preach with the eloquence of my brother Adams." So this first of the Streeters, of whom we have had five in our ministry, with great joy consecrated all his eloquence to the spread of the new faith.

But next to John Murray, the greatest man at that Oxford meeting was Elhanan Winchester. This man deserves a whole volume by himself. "He was a man of peculiar gifts and of wonderful and commanding influence." Elhanan was born in Brookline, Mass., in 1751, the oldest of fifteen children. He was a child of feeble body, never being physically well in his whole short life, but he had a marvellous brain. He was able to read anything in the English language when he was five years old. In one evening with a Latin Grammar he prepared himself to recite with a class that had been at the work for several weeks. The long church service of that time was a severe trial to the nervous child, and his father sternly charged him to sit still, look at the minister, and remember the text. But Elhanan had the wandering eyes, as usual, and when they reached home his sorely vexed father sharply called him to account. But the child told his surprised parent the text, the heads of the sermon, and most of the treatment verbatim, then went on and told how many people were present, and who they were, and the number of beams, posts, braces, and panes of glass there were in the meeting-house. He was a child that puzzled the doctors, both hearing and asking them questions. He had good knowledge of Latin, Greek, and Hebrew; and some one said of him, "Had this surprising man's industry been equal to his retention, he would now rank with the most knowing ones of the age."

When nineteen he joined the Baptist Church, and when twenty they ordained him as a preacher. He was at variance with his brethren on the question of close communion, but not at that time on any other point. In 1778, having been a preacher some seven or eight years, Winchester fell in with a copy of the book that De Benneville had published, Paul Siegvolk's "Everlasting Gospel," and the seed thus sown, slowly began to grow in his mind. That summer he spent in South Carolina, and devoted himself to preaching to the slaves with remarkable success. From time to time he fell in with others who had seen Siegvolk's book, and he also read "The Restitution of All Things" by Mr. Stonehouse. Gradually it became known that Mr. Winchester was reading these books, and the storm began to gather round his head. The opposition and attacks put on him the necessity of defending his ground or abandoning it; and so, turning his whole mind to the matter, he was soon a firm believer in Universalism. He went and visited De Benneville, and was much strengthened in his views. So the great mind came into the light, and he preached his first Universalist sermon about 1781.

He and his sympathizers were expelled from the Baptist communion, and soon after organized "The Society of Universal Baptists" in Philadelphia. We have existing to-day a sermon preached by Mr. Winchester at this time — 1782 — on "The Outcasts Comforted." "To the members of the Baptist Church who have been rejected by their brethren for holding the doctrine of the final restitution of all things."

Mr. Winchester went to London in 1787, remaining until 1794, and during this absence he constantly preached and published his Universalist ideas. On his return to America, he preached in Philadelphia and in New York for about two years. Winchester and Murray did not agree in some of their opinions, and so their relations were not always harmonious, although in time they came to highly esteem each other. Winchester published many books and pamphlets, and prepared a hymn book, writing some of the hymns himself.

But the brilliant spirit was too much for the frail body, and Mr. Winchester felt death approaching. His last days were filled with strenuous labor to provide for his beloved wife. In October, 1796, he was in Hartford, Conn. Having dined, he sauntered out to view the town. Observing a funeral procession, he joined it, and entered the enclosure of the dead. The assemblage was large, and the scene to him solemn and affecting. Addresses at the grave were then of frequent occurrence. The place and occasion induced in him a strong desire to speak to his dying fellow-men. The coffin was just lowered into its earthly receptacle, when he arrested the attention of the multitude by breaking forth in the sublime words of Jesus to the afflicted sisters of Lazarus, "I am the resurrection and the life." The effect was electric. A strain of almost supernatural eloquence now saluted the ear, and engaged the eager gaze of the spellbound throng. The stranger's manner, his clerical habit, and the sepulchral hue of his countenance, conspired to agitate their hearts with various and indescribable emotions; and the tearful eyes of many gave evidence to the power of his remarks. When he ceased to speak, the inquiries, "Who is he?" "Whence came he?" broke spontaneously from every lip. The result of this strangely impressive scene was that certain Universalists in Hartford were not long in finding out Mr. Winchester, and he preached the rest of his brief life in that city. His pastorate was less than a year, however, and in 1797 the strong soul departed in triumph and in joy.

His body lies buried in one of Hartford's old cemeteries. In 1802 the Convention ordered a stone to be erected at his grave, with this inscription: —

"The General Convention of Universal Churches, in Memory of their dear departed brother, Elhanan Winchester, erected this stone. He died April 18th, 1797, Aged 46 years.

" 'Twas thine to preach, with animated zeal,
   The glories of the restitution morn,
 When sin, death, hell the power of Christ shall feel,
   And Light, Life, Immortality be born."

The Hartford Sunday-school a few years ago honored itself by putting in good order the cemetery lot where this great preacher's frail body was laid.

This chapter must not end without making mention of one great layman who was a strong personal friend of both Murray and Winchester, and a pronounced Universalist. Benjamin Rush, M.D., was a great name at this period. Dr. Rush was a signer of the Declaration of Independence, and in all ways an ardent patriot. He published more than fifty volumes on Medicine and Temperance. Dr. Rush had much to do with shaping the Articles of Faith and Plan of Church Government, adopted by the Philadelphia Convention spoken of in another place.

CHAPTER V.

THE THEOLOGY OF JOHN MURRAY.

Theology is a dry subject to most young people, but at least a little of it must be understood if one would follow intelligently the history of our denomination. Our Church Fathers were very vigorous theologians, and their children ought to have some of the same spirit. Some say that theology is "dry bones," but bones have their place. A body all bones is ugly, but a body with no bones is limp. Let us be neither ugly nor limp. Religion is the "Life of God in the Soul of Man." Theology is an effort to state the facts about religion in a logical, systematic way. Religion with no theology is mere sentimentalism, and theology without religion is cold. As we like to see the bones covered with the graceful outlines of the flesh, and know that beneath them there is a beating heart and warm red blood, so let us keep our theology and our religion similarly related.

The theology of our Church may be studied in three stages. The first of these is the John Murray stage, the second is the Hosea Ballou stage, and the third is the modern or present

stage. Here let us study the theology of John
Murray. James Relly, the London preacher
under whom Murray was converted, became the
leader of a school known as Rellyans. The
Gloucester people who called Murray to be their
pastor were Rellyans, and Murray was a Rellyan. What was a "Rellyan"? To answer this
question, we must dip a little into theology as
it was in Relly's day. The theology that we
need to study is the various attempts that have
been made to answer the question, "Why did
Jesus die on the Cross?" The idea was that
God in some way, known only to him, made
Adam the mystical head of the human race, so
whatever Adam did, the race did. When Adam
fell, of course then the whole race of man fell
with him. The human race, then, by Adam's
fall is banished, depraved, and lost under the
wrath of God.

Jesus on the Cross died for this lost race.
Some said that when the race fell in Adam, it
came into the possession of Satan, and that
Jesus paid Satan a ransom in order to induce
him to let all who would accept that ransom
come back to God. Others said that God was
angry with this fallen race, and that Jesus died
to appease this anger. Still others said that
when man sinned, he sinned against an infinite
being, and so broke an infinite law, and so deserved infinite punishment, and that Jesus on

the Cross suffered this infinite punishment to pay this infinite debt. These various theories were called theories of the atonement, or of the work of Jesus on the Cross.

So the theologians read the meaning of the death of Jesus: it paid a ransom to Satan, it appeased an angry God, it paid an infinite debt. In regard to the effect of this atonement, there were two views.

One view was, that God in his infinite pleasure chose a fixed portion of the race from the foundation of the world to be saved. This was the "elect." The rest were the "non-elect," chosen to be lost. Jesus died only for the elect. This is Calvinism. Others held that Jesus died for the whole race, and that as many would be saved as accepted before death the atonement made for them. This is Arminianism, and is held by the Methodists. These Arminians believed in a universal redemption made by Jesus, but not in universal salvation, because some died without accepting that redemption offered, and so were lost.

Now for our question, "What is Rellyanism?" Relly believed that Jesus died for all, and so all were saved. Relly held the theology we have described exactly as all Christians of his day did. He believed in a lost, fallen race, an offended God, the need of redemption, as did all in his day. He differed from them all simply in this. Jesus died for all, therefore the debt is paid for all. All are therefore saved. He accepted the orthodox premises, but drew from them Universalist conclusions. Exactly as Adam was the first mystical head of the race, and all were lost in him whether they knew it or not, so is Jesus the second mystical head of the race, and all are saved in him whether they know it or not. There is a mystical "*union*" between Jesus and each soul which makes the act of Jesus his act. This doctrine was known as Relly's "Union," and this name was given to Relly's book. The Rellyan Universalist was indignant if any one pushed his theory so far as to ask, "If everyone is saved, why preach?" The ready reply was, that while every one was saved, only a few knew it, and the preacher was the man sent to tell all of them the good news. It is clear now why Murray said universal "Restoration" or "Restitution" or "Redemption." He believed, as all Christians of his day did, that the race was lost or fallen, or given over to Satan, by Adam's fall, whether they knew it or not, and that they needed to be restored or redeemed. Jesus on the Cross made a Universal restoration, and all are redeemed or restored whether they know it or not.

John Murray up to about 1778, or after he had been some time at Gloucester, often preached his premises, and left his hearers to draw their own conclusions, and so had access to many pulpits, and fellowship with many preachers, that he would not have had if it had been known that he drew Universalist conclusions from their premises. Many have regarded this as a defect in Murray's character, but he defended himself by saying that it was better that the new light should dawn gradually. This is the reason why so many orthodox pulpits were open to him during his first years in America. Later he became more pronounced, and left no doubt as to his conclusions, and then pulpits once friendly were closed to him, and persecutions thickened.

This Rellyan theology did not last long among us, nor did many beside Murray hold it. Murray was constantly offended with his fellow-preachers because they were not sound in his Rellyan views. About 1787 he wrote, "I do not know of a single preacher in this country, if I except Mr. Tyler, who is with me in sentiment." There were some other Rellyans, however. Mr. Murray regarded Elhanan Winchester, and later Hosea Ballou, as unsound in the faith. Mr. Winchester outgrew the Calvinist theology, and so did Caleb Rich, but Mr. Murray never did. Mr. Winchester thought that the wicked must pass through a long period of burning discipline, perhaps fifty thousand years for the most obdurate, before they could be brought to repentance and consequent salvation.

This was a very radical departure from Mr. Murray's view, that as Adam's sin condemned all, whether they knew it or not, so Jesus's blood saved all, whether they knew it or not. Murray said that Winchester taught salvation by discipline, while the Bible taught salvation by the blood of Jesus.

In 1815, at John Murray's death, Mr. Mitchell, who had been for a time his assistant pastor in Boston, was in charge of a parish in New York. Mr. Mitchell was perhaps the last of the Rellyans among us. He would have no fellowship with other Universalists, because they had departed from Relly. Mr. Mitchell would hardly recognize Dr. Sawyer when he became pastor of the old Orchard Street Church in New York; and on his death-bed he charged his children to have nothing to do with the Universalist Church, so wholly gone over to radicalism. So sore was that faithful spirit, as has been many another since, to see the children outgrow the fathers.

Thus we see how John Murray was a Rellyan, and not the father of our present theology. He lived and died holding strongly and advocating mightily our great conclusion, although he reached that conclusion by a way long since outgrown by us. To the same port that Murray reached in his little brig, passengers now come by the mighty Cunarder; so to his same theological conclusion do many come, but by a way

The Theology of John Murray. 47

he could not see. John Murray is entitled to be called the pioneer of our faith, the father of our organized Church in America, and so let him be forever affectionately remembered and highly honored among us.

CHAPTER VI.

HOSEA BALLOU.

About the time that John Murray, sad-hearted and lonely, was preaching his first sermons in America, a man-child was born in a little farmhouse up in New Hampshire, and named Hosea Ballou. The town was Richmond, the date April 30, 1771. Hosea's father was a Baptist minister; and as this was the eleventh baby that had come to him, the arrival probably created no remarkable sensation. But this baby grew to be a strong man with a clear idea, who has ruled in this world as very few men have. If we limit a man's influence to those who know him and acknowledge him, then Hosea Ballou's influence is not wide; but if we insist that a man's influence is as wide as the reach of the man's supreme idea, then his influence has been surpassed by very few.

When the child was two years old, his mother died, and the baby lost the best thing out of his life. Some women have had an easier time than this mother had, but few have done more for the world. With her it has become pretty nearly true that "the hand that rocks the cradle rules the world."

Her youngest son, as we have just said, was Hosea Ballou. Her second son was Benjamin Ballou; and Benjamin Ballou was the grandfather of Rev. Hosea Ballou, D.D., often known among us as Hosea Ballou 2d. The reader may, if he chooses, figure out the relation that "Father" Ballou was to Dr. Ballou, but he must never confuse the two great leaders.

We have had three biographies of Hosea Ballou: one by his youngest son, Maturin Ballou; another by his most ardent disciple, Thomas Whittemore; and another by Rev. O. F. Safford, D.D. The first two named are out of print. The last-named book, by Dr. Safford, can be had from the Publishing House for one dollar; and we hardly know where a dollar will buy a more readable volume.

With so good a biography so easily reached, we attempt no full life of Hosea Ballou here. We note only the barest outline of a singularly full and rich career.

Our motherless lad spent his formative years in a home of poverty, but it never was degrading poverty. It was the kind of poverty that builds up fibre, and not the kind that deteriorates it. His father was a very good man, who did all that he possibly could for his children. Hard labor was laid upon them all by necessity, but many worse things than that come to a lad. Schools were impossible, with the exception of so few weeks that they are hardly worth making note of.

But ignorance was also impossible, and intelligence of a very vigorous sort was encouraged. It was low living, but high thinking. The religious atmosphere was Calvinism, and it was Calvinism that took itself seriously. The formula, "No matter what you believe," had not yet been discovered. As a matter of fact, nothing else whatever was of any importance except what you believed. It was that, and that only, that saved or lost the soul. Those men did not dally with opinions: they made them conditions of church-fellowship, and the very first conditions.

Here, then, was a stern climate, a stony soil, a stonier theology. Do you say that one would be very glad to outgrow this cheerless place and forget it? Not so. When Hosea Ballou was an old man, the last long journey that he ever took was back to Richmond, N.H., to see once more the spot about which clustered his fondest memories, his most sacred earthly associations.

When Hosea was nineteen, he was immersed in a hole cut through the January ice to the frigid current beneath, and made a member of the Baptist Church. They told him that he would find inner peace if he was a member of the Church; but his eager and inquiring mind could never find the anticipated peace in the Church of his father, eagerly as he sought it. He must think; and to think intelligently and sympathetically about the theology of that day and place, was not peace, but madness.

In desperate straits he turned to his Bible for light, and made a long and deep study of the sacred volume. He was not a casual reader. He dug with sweaty brow, and breath coming fast, for life for himself, and for all his fellow-men. He came out of the study a master of the greatest book in the world, and a Universalist. For this he was, with every possible kindness and consideration, duly expelled from the father's Church. Mr. Ballou was sorely troubled; but, whatever might be true of God, he knew that he was still Hosea's father, no matter what Hosea believed. One day this son was seen reading a book with a special earnestness and absorption that attracted attention. The watchful father asked what book it was, and Hosea told him that it was a Universalist book. He was bidden to put the evil thing away at once, and so obediently hid it in the woodpile. Probably he was not sorry to see his father a little later confiscate the wicked volume, and discover that he had a copy of the New Testament in his hands.

When Hosea was about twenty, he managed to get a few weeks in a private school, and then a term in Chesterfield Academy. Day and night he toiled with such ardor that when he left the Academy he was given a certificate which said that he could teach a common school.

In 1791 he attended the gathering of the General Convention of Universalists at Oxford, Mass. No one noticed him; but the young fellow from the woods was the most important man there for the future of the Church. It was a great occasion for him: for the first time he saw and heard John Murray, Caleb Rich, and Elhanan Winchester. These men awakened in him a desire to preach the great Gospel. He began to hear his "call." He grew up in a minister's home. He had no idea that any one could get a living by preaching. To him there was no material gain in the ministry. The only question was as to how he could support himself while he preached. He resolved to teach school through the week, and preach Sundays. He read some theology with his brother David, who had already become a minister. So one Sunday, Hosea Ballou stood up before his friends and neighbors, and tried to preach his first sermon. But his tongue clove to the roof of his mouth, and this man, who was later to sway thousands, now was dumb. His second attempt was also a failure, and his brother and Caleb Rich advised him to stick to his district school. But by most strenuous efforts he gradually came to his own. In various places in Massachusetts and Rhode Island he taught school, and preached Sundays and week-day evenings, when he could find a hearer. He was coming to be known as a sturdy preacher, and a man who knew his Bible.

In 1794 he again attended the Convention, in the same town of Oxford. This time he was better known, as many present had heard him preach, and some of the new parishes or preaching stations reported at that Convention had been established by him. At these early Conventions, the closing sermon was the event of all. In this effort the preacher brought to a focus all that had been said by others, driving it home with all the eloquence at his command.

On this occasion, Elhanan Winchester was to preach this closing sermon, and he was easily king of them all at that task. Joab Young and Hosea Ballou were in the pulpit with Mr. Winchester. Did any one present in that hour know that it was given him to witness one of the most impressive events in our history? Mr. Winchester was an impulsive man, and often inspired. That day, as he preached on our splendid faith and the new fields opening before the Church, and the urgent need of reapers for these whitening harvests, his words began to sound like an ordination sermon. At the impressive climax of his eloquence, he took the

Bible, and pressing it against young Ballou's breast, said, "Brother Ballou, I press to your heart the written Jehovah." Then in his own impressive style he turned to the other occupant of the desk, and said, "Charge him, Brother Young." Upon which, Mr. Young quickly rose, and said, "I charge you, young brother, preach the word." The congregation was profoundly stirred, and every heart indorsed this impromptu ordination. Later, in those days of theological battle, this ordination was questioned; and so in 1803 Mr. Ballou was ordained again, with an eye to all the legal details.

In 1796 Hosea Ballou married Miss Ruth Washburn, and settled in Dana, Mass. It now began to appear that the pulpit that Hosea Ballou was in would be our strongest pulpit; and so, under the law of survival of the fittest, he started for Boston. He did not get to the metropolis at one step, however. Between Dana and Boston he had pastorates at Barnard, Portsmouth, and Salem.

In 1817, two years after John Murray's death, Hosea Ballou became pastor of the Second Society of Boston, while Rev. Paul Dean succeeded Mr. Murray in the First Church. The labors of Mr. Ballou in that Second Church during the years of his prime seem to us almost beyond belief. Three sermons every Sunday to a congregation expecting great preaching; preaching all over New England on week-day evenings; arguments and debates, oral and written, almost without number; work in the editor's chair, — verily, this man must have had a constitution like the hills of his native State, to have endured all the labors he carried on. And yet no one ever saw Mr. Ballou in a hurry, so the report runs. Dr. Safford makes a pen-picture of Hosea Ballou in the days of his power, preaching in a farmhouse on a week-day evening to an assembly of the neighbors, that makes a young Universalist, reading the words, feel as if he himself was present, and listening to the great preacher.

Hosea Ballou spent the rest of his life in Boston. As his strength failed with advancing years, assistant pastors were provided to lighten his burdens. Rev. T. C. Adams, then Rev. H. B. Soule, after him Rev. J. H. Chapin, and finally Rev. A. A. Miner, were at different times colleagues of Hosea Ballou.

During all these declining years he was held in increasing love and honor among us, finally dying in 1852, more than eighty-one years of age. He was the greatest man in the Universalist Church.

CHAPTER VII.

THE THEOLOGY OF HOSEA BALLOU.

The first stage of our theological development has been spoken of as the Rellyan or John Murray stage. Here the theme is our second or Hosea Ballou stage. As has been said, Hosea Ballou was a great popular preacher; but yet his chief fame among us is as a theologian.

In 1901, at the Universalist General Convention in Buffalo, N.Y., Rev. John Coleman Adams, D.D., chose for the theme of his masterly Occasional Sermon, "Hosea Ballou and the Gospel Renaissance of the Nineteenth Century." This sermon in pamphlet form can be had from the Publishing House, and it throws a flood of light on the topic of this chapter.

Ballou was the people's preacher far more for his matter than for his manner. Theology in that day was a dank wilderness, and everybody wanted to hear Ballou because he had the only ray of sunshine that had yet penetrated that wilderness. He was a great preacher because he had a preachable theology, and made it so clear and reasonable that everybody understood it. "His logic was as simple as the talk of a child, yet strong as the tread of a giant." In him "the common people heard themselves thinking aloud." Dr. Adams compares Hosea Ballou and Abraham Lincoln, and finds a striking resemblance. He had the sweet reasonableness of the Gospels. True, he was a tremendous controversialist, but he was so manly and so fair that strong men liked him all the better for that. They needed fighters in those days, as indeed they do in all days.

In 1804 Mr. Ballou published his first book, — the "Notes on the Parables." This book shows that he is still more or less a Rellyan, and there are touches of fantastic interpretations of Scripture in it; but it shows a sturdy mind, a wonderful mind when you reflect that it had had no human teacher, dealing with the parables according to some of the principles that every scholar uses to-day.

It was a year later, however, that Hosea Ballou published his epoch-making book, — "A Treatise on Atonement." In this famous book the principles are laid down that make Hosea Ballou the father of our Universalist theology. It may be said that it makes him the father of Unitarian theology also, since here he attacks the doctrine of the Trinity, and asserts the Unity and supremacy of God, ten years before the American Unitarian denomination existed.

Note how he deals with the doctrine of the trinity. First he states it as follows: "They all contend, that the Godhead consists of *three distinct persons*, viz., Father, Son, and Holy Ghost; that these *distinct* persons are equal in power and glory, and eternally and essentially one. For the sake of the argument, then, I admit the foregoing statement of the character of Christ to be just; and then I contend, that if he be the Son of God, he is the Son of himself, and is his own father; that he is no more the Son of God than God is his Son. If Jesus Christ were really God, it must be argued that God really died. Again, if the Godhead really consists of three distinct persons, and each of these persons be infinite, the whole Godhead amounts to the amazing sum of infinity multiplied by three. If it is said that neither of these three persons alone is infinite, I say the three together, with the addition of a million more such, would not make an infinite being." Ballou goes on at length to prove from Scripture that Jesus is not God, but a created dependent being. Jesus is exalted above other men because God his Father anointed him to be so. Then this book goes on with clearest phrase and homely illustrations to talk about these ideas of the atonement that we described a few pages back. He takes the idea that sin has broken an infinite law, and so demands an infinite sacrifice to satisfy infinite justice. He comments this way on it: "Divines of the greatest ability have drained the last faculty of invention, in plodding through the dark regions of metaphysics, to bring up a Samuel to explain the solecism of satisfying an *infinite* dissatisfaction."

So with clear talk he makes it impossible for any one to believe any of the theories of atonement held by the Christian world of that day. Jesus did not die to pay a ransom to Satan, for Satan never got possession of the race so God had to pay a ransom to get it back. Jesus did not die to appease infinite anger, for the infinite God always loved the world. Now in his book Mr. Ballou passes to the positive answer to the question of the meaning of the death of Jesus. It was not to effect a change in God. God needed not to be changed. It was to change man. Man was lost, blind, rebellious, and he needed to be reconciled to God. God did not need to be reconciled to man. Jesus's life and death are the message the infinite loving heart of God sends to his children to plead with them to come home. Does it seem to you that everybody holds this now? All honor, then, to the clear brain that thought it all out when nobody believed it, and the brave tongue that declared it like a voice crying in the wilderness.

John Murray was strongly opposed to this new theology, so destructive of his Calvinistic and trinitarian and mystical ideas. In 1798, some years before the appearance of the "Treatise," Mr. Murray was troubled about the unsound theology of young Ballou. During this year Mr. Murray, having occasion to be absent from Boston, invited Hosea Ballou to occupy his pulpit for ten Sundays. The invitation was accepted, although Mr. Murray frankly informed the "supply" that his views on theology were not entirely satisfactory. So Hosea Ballou came to Boston and preached his sermons. At the close of the last one, Mrs. Murray, who had listened to them all with an ear keen for heresy, induced a friend to stand up and say to the congregation, "I wish to give notice that the doctrine which has been preached here to-day is not the doctrine that is usually preached in this house." The authorities do not agree as to the retort Mr. Ballou made, but it is very certain, that, whatever Mr. Ballou's theology was in the particular sermon preached that day, before many years had passed, his theology was indeed not that "usually preached in that place."

There was much indignation at the time over Mrs. Murray's public announcement, and the parish committee called on Mr. Ballou, and expressed regret. Several, who were much impressed by Mr. Ballou's opinions and his clear way of putting them, hinted that if he would move to Boston they would build a church for him. "I cannot," he said, "do anything to injure Brother Murray nor the beloved society to which he ministers."

So for twenty years longer Boston heard Rellyan Universalism, until 1817, when the School Street Church was built, and Hosea Ballou put into its pulpit.

Beside this explanation of the atonement, another idea of Hosea Ballou's has come to have a particular interest to us to-day in defending our faith. Hosea Ballou believed in the Sovereignty of God. No Calvinist believed in this idea more than Ballou did. Jonathan Edwards made God absolute sovereign, but a sovereign so terrible in wrath and cruelty that man fell crushed before him. Hosea Ballou believed God was an absolute sovereign of infinite love and wisdom. Possibly he believed in this great thought so vigorously that he sometimes made it seem that man was only a puppet moved by a power not himself, and so not responsible for what he did. Usually Ballou did not do this; but if he must sacrifice God's sovereignty or man's freedom, then he forgot man's freedom.

Almost at the beginning of the "Treatise" he says, "If we admit a disappointment to the Supreme Being, even in the smallest matter of consideration, it follows that we have no satisfactory evidence whereby to prove that anything in the whole universe is as the Supreme intended."

Back in the fifties this matter was a fruitful source of debate among us. Thomas Whittemore and I. D. Williamson defended stoutly Ballou's theory of Divine Sovereignty, and Hosea Ballou 2d and Dr. Sawyer spoke for human freedom and responsibility.

After them this capital old question for debating societies seemed to be forgotten, until a recent event has called it all up again for our Church to think of anew. At the Universalist General Convention of 1899 in Boston, Lyman Abbott came, and spoke by special request on "Why I am not a Universalist." The address was in the great editor's best vein, and gave keen pleasure to all who heard it.

Dr. Abbott thought that some would not be saved. He emphatically repudiated all the old reasons for that opinion. These souls are not lost because God decreed it, desired it, refused them a chance, was angry, revengeful. In short, it is not God's fault in any particular that any soul is lost. It is the soul's own choice. Man's will is free, and he may will to go to endless perdition in spite of God. Instantly the old question of the Sovereignty of God *vs.* the Freedom of the Will was up again for discussion and thought. Hosea Ballou's Sovereignty of God was restated, and no doctrine is more needed to-day. The psychology of our day states the doctrine of the will in a way Ballou could not have known. To us the will of man is not an entity, a faculty fenced off by itself, concerning which we can ask, Is it free? To us the will is simply the whole Self willing. And the self, willing, is as much under certain laws as any spiritual fact is. God coerces no man, but God trains and disciplines each man until he wills right. Ballou had no idea of a universe in which mortal man was stronger than God, and able forever to thwart God's will. He believed in a successful God. So this unschooled man from the hills went forth. Says Dr. Adams, "His method was dignified and noble. His spirit was Christian. His practical teaching was wise and effective. He went to the people. He traversed New England and New York, preaching wherever a hearing could be had. He argued like Socrates. He pleaded like Paul. He was as serene as the firmament."

So Hosea Ballou laid the enduring foundation for the theology of our Church and for the theology of all those who think things through.

CHAPTER VIII.

THE RESTORATION CONTROVERSY.

In the year 1817 Hosea Ballou sent to Rev. Edward Turner, the Universalist pastor at Charlestown, a friendly challenge to debate with him the question whether the Scriptures teach the doctrine of future punishment or not. This is the only debate that Mr. Ballou ever went into that we wish he had kept out of. It connected his name with a theory that cannot be true. He told Mr. Turner to take either side that he chose, leaving him to advocate the other; but he well knew which side Mr. Turner would take. Mr. Turner chose to defend the idea that the Scriptures do teach some future punishment, which will go on until the last sinful soul is disciplined to repentance, and then will end.

Those who followed Mr. Turner, some of them at least, chose the name Restorationists instead of Universalists. They believed in future but not in endless punishment. Mr. Ballou asserted that the Scriptures in no place teach future punishment. His final word on the matter was, that as regards sin, "its biblical history begins and ends in the flesh." It is not death that saves the sinner; but, on the instant the soul reaches the other life, it will "behold such heavenly illumination as will cause a glad forgetfulness of things behind and a pressing forward to the things before." So, in the minds of many people the great name of Hosea Ballou stands identified with a scheme which some one with more wit than knowledge has dubbed "Death and Glory."

This opinion of Mr. Ballou's has been more caricatured than any other opinion ever attributed to us. As an opinion, it appears fantastic and absurd; and because Hosea Ballou held one such opinion, many have dismissed him contemptuously, and have never understood his system of theology at all. For Hosea Ballou did have a system of theology, which was sound, even if he did hold one idea that is not sound.

The doctrine of no future punishment was really a very unimportant factor in Mr. Ballou's system, and, as he stated it, did violence to no moral law. He declared that the essential thing was to believe that punishment would go on until it had completely done its work. The question of just how long that would take was not essential. It is nevertheless greatly to be regretted that he, apparently for no purpose whatever save to find vent for his energy as a debater, should ever have gone into a discussion that forced him to appear as an advocate of no future punishment. It has greatly lessened and postponed his influence in the world. Of course there must have been some discussion among the brethren about future punishment, before 1817, or the debate would not have been thought of. We find indeed that Father Rich had by a fanciful interpretation of Scripture drawn the conclusion that the history of sin ends in flesh and blood. This view became a ground of offence against us very early in our history. As early as 1791 the Philadelphia Convention was urged to define the position of the Universalist Church on the question of future punishment. The Convention responded to the request with this statement of belief: —

"Unbelievers do die in their sins; such will not be purged from their sins or unbelief by death, but necessarily must appear in the next state under all that darkness, fear, torment, and conscious guilt, which is the natural consequence of unbelief of the truth. What may be the degree or duration of this state of unbelief and misery, we know not. But this we know, that it hath one uniform and invariable end; namely, the good of the creature."

Oh that some good angel had put it into the minds of all the fathers to let this excellent statement stand! But that was not to be; and so in 1817 the debaters fall to, to determine exactly how long punishment would have to endure to make all men good. Really, it is not fair to let this little by-play so occupy our attention that we forget the noble system of theology the debaters held. It is a fact that the question of the exact time of the duration of punishment is of no great importance. The important thing is to believe that punishment will go on until it has accomplished its purpose, and on that important thing all were in entire harmony. The debate ran on in the shape of fourteen letters, that were published in our denominational paper, the "Gospel Visitant." Then the contest closed, not because either side surrendered, or claimed the victory, but because a merciful Providence ordained that the "Visitant" should cease to be published at that point. Probably, measured by the merits of the debate, Mr. Ballou won, as Mr. Turner at one point confessed that he was not much of an "argumentator;" but measured by the merits of the question, Mr. Ballou lost, and has in some measure ever since been giving account for idle words in an idle debate. Our Church has suffered in reputation, and many merely nominal Universalists have suffered in character from the popular notion that we thought there was no punishment after death. Hosea Ballou's orthodox opponents thought that all punishment was postponed until after death, and then it was endless. It is to be much regretted that he should even appear to lend his name to a doctrine as extreme in one way as the doctrine he combated was the other way, that all punishment is in this life.

The details of the bitterness that grew out of this debate we need not recall here, but some phases of it ought to be understood in defence of Hosea Ballou. Mr. Turner raised the question as to whether death does work a moral change in a man and save him. Mr. Ballou at once declined to answer any question in that form. He stoutly affirmed that "at the dissolution of the natural corruptible body, the Saviour of sinners, who has conquered death, may do what death could not effect, and clothe the subject of his grace in his right mind, as he did the man among the tombs." It is not death, but the Saviour, that saves sinners. "Never," he wrote to Dr. Channing, "did we ascribe the power of cleansing from sin to anything but that which the Scriptures mean by the 'blood of the Lamb.'"

In 1819 Mr. Ballou became editor of the "Universalist Magazine," and it seemed to be expected that he would use its columns to exploit his theory of no punishment after death. Instead of this expected course, however, he was so silent about the matter that his readers complained that they could not tell what he believed on that point. They urged him to declare himself openly. He did so declare himself, asserting that in principle it makes no difference whatever whether a man believes in limited future punishment or no future punishment. He said, "Two brothers may be perfectly agreed about the parent. They both believe that he will give them all the instruction needed, and yet may entertain different views about time and place. One may think that they are to be kept at school until they are eighteen, the other that they are to be kept under tutors a year longer, yet both may believe that their father knows best. He who believes that all suffering ends with this mortal state, and he who believes that it ends at the expiration of any other period, differ only as respects time, and not as respects principle." Why did not Mr. Ballou write this luminous letter to Mr. Turner at the start, and decline to waste precious time and strength, and stir up contention, and alienate brethren, when, as he himself declared, no principle was involved? But that sweet reasonableness was not then to be.

The hot-headed youngsters, Thomas Whittemore for no future punishment, and Adin Ballou for limited future punishment, each followed by many doughty warriors, entered the lists. So it came to pass that in 1831, convinced that they were unjustly treated, a little company gathered at Mendon, Mass., and formally seceded from our Church, taking the name, "The Massachusetts Association of Universal Restorationists." They adopted the Winchester Confession, adding to it the words, "We believe in retribution beyond death." About twenty clergymen, we do not know how many laymen, joined this Restorationists' movement. This number by no means represented all those who believed in limited future punishment: it simply is the number that thought the matter important enough to warrant secession. Adin Ballou, the leading spirit in the exodus, said that there was hot work for a few years. Gradually, however, everybody recovered normal temperature; and after holding annual Conventions for about ten years, the last one being in 1841, the Restorationists disappeared as a separate sect. To-day we do not use the word "Restorationist" to describe our opinions, as that word implies that the race was lost in Adam, and is to be restored to some condition it has once been in and lost by that fall. This we do not believe. The world is not being restored to something it had and lost, but is being led on to a high estate yet to be realized. But, as regards the doctrine of future punishment, the Restorationists completely won the field, and hold the ground to-day in all our Church.

CHAPTER IX.

SOME OTHER LEADERS.

Thus far our history has been related closely to two great names, John Murray and Hosea Ballou. It cannot be written in this fashion any further, for after Ballou, or even in his time, it becomes a history of organizations and institutions rather than of individuals. Yet, beside Hosea Ballou and after him, there stood a company of strong leaders whom the young Universalist ought to know all about. The clear-brained Scotchman, Walter Balfour, was such a leader. He was born in 1776, six years after Hosea Ballou, in Scotland. From youth he was very thoughtful and very honest. When a thing seemed to him to be true, he fearlessly stood for it. He obeyed God, as God spoke to him in the inner voice.

A rich man in Scotland determined to devote a part of his fortune to the spread of the gospel in his native land, and for this purpose chose twenty of the most promising young men available, to educate for the ministry. Balfour was one of the twenty. Scotland never believed in an ignorant ministry, and the young men were put in the very best schools. In 1806 we find the young man, then thirty years old, in America, living in Charlestown, and preaching to a small company of people in a hall, who appreciated him very highly. He preached without compensation, supporting himself and his family by keeping a small store.

So we find him up to about 1812 preaching the old Scotch theology without a question as to its truth. About this time the great Trinitarian-Unitarian controversy came on, and Dr. Channing for the Unitarians, and Prof. Moses Stuart for the Trinitarians, entered the field. Among many things Channing said, "Jesus is not God, because the Bible in no case teaches that we are to render spiritual worship unto Christ." Prof. Stuart replied that the New Testament does teach us to worship Christ, and quoted as proof the text in Philippians, "That at the name of Jesus every knee should bow, of things in heaven, and things in earth, and things under the earth; and that every tongue should confess that Jesus Christ is Lord." He said, "Things in heaven, earth, and under the earth is a common periphrasis of the Hebrew and New Testament writers for the Universe. What can be meant by this if spiritual worship is not meant?" Balfour was following the controversy with intense interest, and this great statement of Prof. Stuart worked profoundly in his mind. The whole Universe rendering spiritual worship to Christ? How, then, can the doctrine of endless punishment be true? He wrote letter after letter to Mr. Stuart, imploring him to explain this matter to him. No answer being given to his anxious inquiry, he was forced into the study of the whole question for himself. The result was that he became a Universalist. These letters to Moses Stuart, with further inquiries that grew out of that study, make two books, that are known among us as "Balfour's Inquiry." It may be doubted if any books published in that half of the century converted as many to our faith as did these "Inquiries." To this day it is difficult to see how one could read them and not accept their main conclusion. Thousands owe to Walter Balfour their release from error's chains.

Another famous man among us was Thomas Whittemore. He was born in Boston, Jan. 1, 1800, and was an apprentice to a shoemaker when Hosea Ballou came to Boston. He went to hear the great man preach, and by and by went into his study to learn how to preach himself. He was a credit to his teacher, and after a while it came to pass that when the master could not be present, the next choice would be Thomas Whittemore. He was mighty in the pulpit. Some one who heard him one summer day in a village church in Vermont tells how in the very midst of one of Whittemore's thrilling sermons a little bird flew in at the open window and fluttered wildly about the room. Soon the frightened bird had the attention of the audience. Whittemore stopped and waited until the bird was released. Could he take up that broken thread, and go on at the exalted pitch he was in when interrupted? The preacher, when quiet was restored, told the old Norse tale of the warriors at their rude feast in their hall, and the bird coming in from out the storm and flying across the room, passing out into the darkness on the other side; and how one warrior then had spoken of human life as being like the flight of this bird. It comes out of the darkness, is a moment within our ken, and then passes into the darkness. Whittemore used this story with most impressive effect, and thus turned into victory an incident that would have been defeat to a less ready man.

All the while that Whittemore was making this reputation as a preacher, he was editor of our Church paper that succeeded Mr. Ballou's "Universalist Magazine." Whittemore named the new paper the "Trumpet," and he never let it give any uncertain sound during the thirty-three years he edited it. This marvellous man wrote ten books and scores of pamphlets, and was the only Universalist minister who was ever president of a bank and of a railroad. He was also a member of the Massachusetts Legislature. "Picturesque, unforgettable man, in intensity and activity almost miraculous."

There is a long list of men who were our leaders, of whom no separate biography has been written. Lucius R. Paige, who gave us our only complete Commentary, is one of these. Thomas Baldwin Thayer, author of "The Theology of Universalism" and "Over the River," has instructed and comforted a host of souls as they passed along life's way. Abel C. Thomas wrote "A Century of Universalism," and left a beautiful memory with us. John G. Adams, W. S. Balch, I. D. Williamson, E. G. Brooks, with his stirring words in his volume "Our New Departure," Sylvanus Cobb, Stephen R. Smith, A. B. Grosh, Ebenezer Fisher, George H. Emerson, George W. Montgomery, J. M. Austin, and the Skinners are names which call up stirring memories in many yet with us. Hosea Ballou 2d, our great scholar, and Dr. Chapin, the greatest orator of our Church, — shall we not say of any Church? — are names that will never die. A Church can never be local nor small that remembers Ryder, Miner, Sawyer, and Pullman. What a splendid list the young Universalist has in such laymen as Tufts, Ropes, Packard, Gunn, Lombard, Dean, Harsen, Thomas and Mary Goddard, Craig, Buchtel, Throop, Swan, John D.

W. Joy, and Newton Talbot, not to speak of the living!

These are some of our saints: there are hosts of others. Every parish among us can easily add to this list. It is devoutly hoped that this will be something more than a list of empty names to our young people. They are all worthy of study until they call up in every mind living pictures of brave and loyal workers on our walls, with sword and trowel in hand. Nothing could be better for a winter's course of study than the stories of the life and works of these leaders. Of some there are full biographies: for the lives of others of them, one must go over the files of our periodicals. All these great leaders are, however, best studied in connection with some organized interest of our Church, some phase of our institutional life. Some of them made great pulpits, some made great Sunday-schools, some made our literature better, some toiled to organize our Conventions, some have stood for our schools and our missions. Our history must now deal with these organizations and institutions rather than with individuals.

CHAPTER X.

THE UNIVERSALIST SOCIETIES, PARISHES, AND CHURCHES.

THE organized Universalist denomination is made up of four factors. These factors are the individual, the local society parish or Church, the State Conventions, and the General Conventions.

We shall have a strong working, growing denomination when these four factors are properly coördinated, each being vitally connected and related to all the other factors. The problem for us is, as our history proves that it has always been, to bring about this efficient coördination of these factors. Some individuals are Universalists, they say, but will have nothing to do with the other three factors. Many will interest themselves in the local society parish or Church, who know nothing and care less about the State Conventions. To a still larger number the General Convention is only a vague name. Our people do not hold the true view of the connection between individual welfare and a strong centralized organization. We fix our attention on the individual and forget the organization. We do very poor team-work because everybody is bound to do as he pleases, and will not listen to the captain. Now it has always been true, and is particularly true to-day, that the work of the world will be done by some compact efficient organization, that controls individuals enough to make them lift and act together, but not so much as to destroy individual initiative and responsibility. For the first hundred years of our history we bungled wretchedly on this matter of effective organization. It is only within the last thirty-five years that any sort of successful attempt has been made toward efficient organization of our forces.

Even yet it is probably true that there are more men who hold our Universalist opinions who are entirely outside of our organization, than there are who are vitally connected with it. If history has any voice to young Universalists, it is, "Join the nearest Church and parish, be an active member, go to the State Convention, take an active part, go to the Biennial General Convention, keep informed about your denomination, be a part of it." This chapter is concerned with the second factor in our denominational organization, the society or the parish or the Church. This is the smallest grouping of individuals, the local group.

The Universalist Societies.

There is no fixed line between the three names given to this local group. Up to about 1870 the commonest name of these groups was "Societies." Generally to-day we speak of them as parishes and Churches. The parish is the business organization, the Church is the religious organization distinctively. Generally, any one who attends and contributes toward the support of local services is a parish member, while a Church member is one who has been baptized, and who is a communicant at the Lord's table. Usually all Church members are parish members, but unfortunately not all parish members are Church members.

History shows that the society and the parish do not have the vitality nor the staying qualities that the Church has. It is the duty and privilege of every young Universalist to be a live member of the Historic Church of Jesus Christ.

Our first organized society was at Gloucester, Mass. The same year Murray landed at Good Luck, an Englishman brought a copy of Relly's "Union" to Gloucester. The man in New Jersey and the book in Massachusetts were each at work. The book gathered a company and made Rellyans of them before they ever heard of Murray. Then when they did hear of Murray they were prepared to receive him. He came and organized our first American parish in

Gloucester in 1779. That parish took the name, "The Independent Church of Gloucester." It adopted articles of association in which the members agreed to work together under John Murray as long as he preached sound doctrine. At different times thirty-one men and thirty women signed these articles. Neither Murray nor his Gloucester people believed in water baptism, nor did Murray think that the Lord's Supper was obligatory upon believers. He said that Universalists generally adopted it as their most reasonable service, but did not hold themselves in subjection thereto. Very soon after Gloucester organized, we had societies at Oxford, Boston, and other places, until in the year 1800 we had about thirty-five societies scattered from Pennsylvania to Maine, and extending west into New York.

It is useless to attempt figures here, the names society and parish are so vague. Some of these societies were simply occasional gatherings to hear some preacher who chanced along. Many of these meetings were held in groves and schoolhouses, often in halls and barns. Sometimes they built meeting-houses, which would be opened to the occasional preacher and then closed. Few of these really attempted to maintain regular services of public worship, but they are all counted as societies. Some years a large number of these societies would be reported, and everybody would feel encouraged at our growth, but a few years later these so-called societies had vanished like dew before the sun. If only these early preachers had gathered these hearers round the communion table of the Lord, and knit them into Church fellowship, more would have stayed.

An occasional gathering of people to listen to preaching is not a parish. Often the members of these societies went to meeting when they felt like it, contributed little or nothing, saw no use in joining the Church, or in the rites of baptism and communion; and so the society soon passes, and has to be stricken from the list, and it appears that we are losing numbers. The fact is, that scores of these little sporadic gatherings ought never to have been counted as societies.

A careful study of the whole story proves that the enduring, working, building, growing organization is the Church of Christ, and not the mere society or parish. A few extracts from reports of societies read at a Convention in 1792 have a lesson for us; indeed, they may have a modern and familiar sound to some: "The brethren in this place are averse to system, and generally walk as it seemeth right to every man." The result was, as any sensible person might have foreseen, that they walked into oblivion, and our denomination has not had any name in that place. Here is the report from Newport, R.I.: "Those that are at Newport join neither with the world nor with each other. They are afraid of months and of days and of years; and to avoid being tangled with what they deem a yoke of bondage, they keep from even the appearance of assembling at any time." Here is the sufficient answer to the question why we have no Church at Newport. These facts of our history ought to speak with tongues to us to hasten to perfect the coördination of the four factors of our denomination.

We have to-day about a thousand parishes; and out of this number many single societies could be named that have vastly more strength than all we had a hundred years ago, put together, excepting two.

One of our churches that has much significance historically was the old Orchard Street Church in New York City. Dr. T. J. Sawyer went into the Orchard Street Church in April, 1832, and was pastor there until 1845. Then he resigned to take the presidency of Clinton Liberal Institute; but in 1853 he went back to Orchard Street for a second pastorate, which lasted until 1859, when, owing to shifting of population, the old church was sold. The old Orchard Street Church under Dr. Sawyer has passed into our history as the institution noted for making intelligent Universalists, who knew what they believed, and could tell why they believed it. Dr. Sawyer was not averse to discussion and debate, and the very air was electric with attack and defence, controversy and doctrine, during the Orchard Street years. It seems as if there was no time in all those years that Dr. Sawyer did not have at least one public debate on his hands defending his faith. The men and women who stood beside Dr. Sawyer those years were of the sturdiest stuff. Dr. Tuttle says, "The influence of the Church in Orchard Street was mighty and far-reaching. Its emigrants settled in other parts of the city, and in the country to the Mississippi and beyond. Its people were a synonym for soundness and faithfulness; the strength it added to our denomination is beyond estimate." While the Orchard Street Church lost its building on that street, its members were not lost. They were workers and builders wherever they went. "All Souls' Church" in Brooklyn was founded largely by Dr. Sawyer's people, and they are found to this day in many places of our Zion.

Columbus Avenue Church in Boston, formerly the School Street Church, is historically of great interest. Here Hosea Ballou was pastor from 1818 until his death in 1852, easily making this our first Church in influence all those years. In 1846, when Mr. Ballou began to feel the weight of his years, E. H. Chapin, the golden-tongued, became his colleague for two years. In 1848 Dr. A. A. Miner came to this preacher's throne. For more than forty years he ministered to that parish. During most of those years Dr. Miner was the recognized leader of our Church. Here he died with the words on his lips, "Tell the ministers to be faithful."

Hon. H. B. Metcalf, himself a product of the old parish of which it may well be proud, has said that the old School Street Church, now Columbus Avenue Church, furnished the men to establish the "Universalist Sabbath School Union," the "Universalist Publishing House," and the first institution that we had outside the parish that could be called an ecclesiastical institution, "The Massachusetts State Convention of Universalists." They have largely been behind Tufts College and all denominational works.

The Churches in Philadelphia have behind them a rich history, told by A. C. Thomas in his "Century of Universalism." The Church of the Divine Paternity in New York, with the fame of Dr. Chapin built into its walls, and the memory of Dr. Eaton illuminating it, is a centre of commanding influence.

Dr. Ryder and St. Paul's Church of Chicago, Dr. Tuttle and the Churches in Minneapolis, are names of men and places that ought to be familiar words for generations of Universalists.

So from Calais to Spokane, and from Atlanta

to Canada, we have men who are not simply making societies, but who are building on broad and deep and enduring foundations Churches of Jesus Christ. May the day come when every individual who holds the Universalist idea, shall be a consecrated member of the Universalist Church!

CHAPTER XI.

ASSOCIATIONS AND CONVENTIONS.

In the preceding chapter we have spoken of the first two factors of our denomination, the individual and the society, parish, or Church. In this chapter we are to note the grouping of all the societies in one section into an association or into a State Convention, and to note how all the State Conventions at last form a General Convention, the supreme governing body. Many Universalists, as we have seen, have been and are individualists, holding fast to their right to walk alone and do as they please. Gradually some Universalists have become congregationalists, but many have no interest in our denomination beyond that.

Congregationalism is the form of Church Government in which each congregation does as it pleases. In pure congregationalism there is no Pope nor Bishop nor Presbytery nor Synod, nor any other power whatsoever that has any right to dictate to the local congregation. Each congregation is its own ruler. Universalists are strongly biassed toward congregational government. Very early in our history thoughtful men among us saw that great good would come if the con-

Associations and Conventions. 87

gregations of the same section at least would meet annually for consultation, agreement, and to unite in common statements of belief and common tasks. The history of our denomination might easily be written from the point of view of two parties, one of which has always fought and pleaded for centralization, establishment of Conventions with some authority over local parishes, and another party that has opposed or been indifferent to all organization. It seems as if the gain must have been immense if the thirty-five parishes we had in 1800 could have had some mutual understanding and united common endeavor, some superintendency.

John Murray and some other leading spirits greatly desired this, but the most were indifferent, and the difficulties in the way of doing it seemed insurmountable. Believers were separated by great distances, travel was difficult, slow, and expensive, the people were poor, and forced to unremitting toil, and opposition and persecution appalled all but the stoutest hearts. In spite of all obstacles, however, about 1778 Warwick, Jaffrey, and Richmond, in New Hampshire associated themselves together, and agreed to meet annually. This association gave letters of license, and ordination to ministerial applicants. This appears to be our first effort to associate parishes for united action.

In 1783 John Murray wrote to Noah Parker,

proposing an association of all the societies, and this proposal bore fruit in a meeting at Oxford, Mass., Sept. 14, 1785. We have referred to this association in a previous chapter, as consisting of nine laymen from five parishes, and four ministers. This association advised that each society take the same name, "Independent Christian Society, commonly called Universalist;" and it drew up a pattern constitution for all to adopt. Three societies accepted the advice of the association: the other two kept on doing just as they pleased. This Oxford association held three annual meetings, and then died, and we lapsed again to pure congregationalism.

It was 1790 before another attempt was made to associate our societies. A letter was then sent to every known parish, asking that delegates be sent to a convention at which should be considered the question of having "one uniform mode of Divine worship, one method of ordaining suitable persons to the ministry, one consistent way of administering the Lord's Supper, and whatever else may seem desirable when the Convention meets." This Convention, held in Philadelphia, began on the 25th of May, 1790, and continued in session until the 8th of June. This was known as the Philadelphia Convention, and it held twenty annual sessions, ceasing to exist in 1809.

Associations and Conventions. 89

Perhaps this first meeting of the Philadelphia Convention, lasting fourteen days, was the longest session any ecclesiastical body among us ever held. They fully appreciated the importance of their task, and took time to do it well. There were seven preachers and ten laymen, representing eight Churches, present. They adopted a creed, referred to later; they formulated a plan of Church government; they agreed that the administration of the ordinances should be left to the individual conscience; they passed some excellent resolutions about the instruction of children, against war, against holding of slaves, and against going to law. Dr. Benjamin Rush took an active part in this Convention.

The real parent of our present General Convention was a gathering which met in Oxford, Mass., Sept. 4, 1793. The records of this meeting are lost; but under slightly varying names this Convention held an annual meeting until 1889, at which date the meetings of the General Convention were made biennial, and so remain. We are not to think, however, of this association as being "General;" almost a hundred years pass before it gets to that.

Thus it happens that for these early years the student of our history has to follow the doings of the Philadelphia Convention, and of this other calling itself a General Convention, and a score or more of Associations. In 1799 the Eastern Association for the District of Maine organized itself. In 1804, Vermont, New Hampshire, and part of New York formed the Northern Association. In 1806 the Western Association appeared, including the remainder of the State of New York. In 1815 the Southern Association was created by Rhode Island and Connecticut parishes. As population increased and societies multiplied, these Associations were cut up into smaller ones, and new ones were created, until the list is too long to print. Many have disappeared, but we still have fifty-seven reported in the Register. For many years each of these Associations assumed the same powers that are now vested in the State and General Conventions. As occasions to call our people together to feel the touch of fellowship and to listen to stirring preaching, these Associations have been, and are still, of great use. But when each had power to legislate for itself regardless of the others, in matters of license, ordination, and discipline, hopeless confusion arose. There was no possible source from which some great plan could emanate to enlist the whole Church in the same enterprise. This government by association was a slight advance on congregationalism, but it was very weak and uncertain. A man who could not get licensed to preach by some Association must have been dull indeed.

Associations and Conventions. 91

Gradually all wise leaders came to see that all the Associations in any State ought to form one State Convention, and that State Convention ought to be the head for that State. Thus in 1828 the five Associations in Maine formed the Maine State Convention. In 1832 New Hampshire and Connecticut did the same. Vermont followed in 1833, and Massachusetts in 1834. In New York it was as late as 1845 before all the Associations would agree to surrender their legislative powers to a State body.

This movement went on until to-day no Association claims any direct legislative power on matters concerning the general Church interests. In twenty-four States the Associations have put all direct ecclesiastical governing power for the State into State Conventions. Thus it appears that we have twenty-four State Conventions. The Province of Ontario has also a Convention. In States where we have not enough parishes to make a Convention, they hold what are called State Conferences, looking toward the time when numbers will warrant the organization of a Convention. We have ten such Conferences reported. Nearly all these State Conventions have invested funds and carry on missionary work each in its own borders.

It appeared that a great step had been taken when we got all our parishes and Associations organized into State Conventions; but it soon appeared that government by State Conventions, while better than that of Associations, was still very bad. The States legislated at cross-purposes. There were no uniform laws for all the denomination. There was no recognized head which could summon all the States to unite in large denominational enterprises. The wise leaders saw more and more clearly that there must be a General Convention with coördinating and directing power over all the States. To effect this has been a long, slow process, and it is still not perfected. In 1830 the Maine State Convention declared itself a "distinct and independent religious body, having the right to transact its own business without the intervention of any other body whatsoever." The New York Convention in the same year adopted the same sentiment. So said nearly all the Conventions then existing. It was the era of State rights in our history. We were twenty or so little denominations, each seeing only itself, and not one Church at all.

Several attempts were made to organize bodies uniting a number of States, before the General Convention had much recognition. The most notable of these attempts was the Northwestern Conference organized in 1860 at Chicago. It included the States of Indiana, Illinois, Iowa, Michigan, Minnesota, Ohio, and Wisconsin. This Conference did not oppose the Conventions, it

Associations and Conventions. 93

reported to the General Convention as a subordinate body. It had an oversight of Church property within its limits, saving thousands of dollars worth by a little timely aid. It raised forty thousand dollars to help build new churches, expended fifteen hundred dollars to aid students in Canton Theological School, and raised a hundred thousand dollars for Lombard University. It gave up its separate existence in 1870 after a career of great usefulness in the West.

Our great leaders, like Dr. Sawyer and Dr. Brooks, raised their voices in a mighty plea to all our people to create one ecclesiastical body, with a reasonable authority over all lesser bodies, and with power to direct all these confused, weak, and scattered parts in all the world. They explained, wrote, spoke, and privately urged the matter, and with them all others who wanted a Universalist Church. In 1860 the matter had gathered headway enough so that a committee was chosen to consider the whole question of the relation between all lesser bodies and the General Convention. But the Civil War came on, everybody forgot all about this committee, nor did they appear to take themselves at all seriously. Occasionally they feebly reported progress, but it did not appear anywhere outside of their report. At last in 1864 a Committee, with Rev. Richard Eddy,

D.D., at the head, proposed a form of constitution clearly defining the powers of the General Convention and the various State Conventions and minor bodies, making the former the real head of the denomination. In 1865 it appeared that the majority of the State Conventions had consented to this proposed form of organization, and in 1866 it was made our accepted Constitution; and our annual mass meeting became for the first time an ecclesiastical body, a real General Convention.

We speak of our Church in America as having been born in 1770 when John Murray came. It might be nearer the truth to say that it was born in 1866 when for the first time we reached the point where we had a denomination with a recognized head and properly related parts.

This Constitution thus adopted in 1866 did not prove to be adequate to the needs of our organization. It was soon seen that it must be broadened and changed. In 1868, only two years after its adoption, Mr. Henry E. Busch placed before the Convention a proposed revision of the whole matter. In 1869 this matter of revision was referred to a committee of five; Rev. E. G. Brooks, Rev. H. W. Rugg, Rev. J. S. Cantwell, J. D. W. Joy, and W. T. Parker composing the committee.

This was a committee of experts, and they gave the important matter put into their hands

Associations and Conventions. 95

very careful study. They held frequent meetings, they consulted widely with our people, they asked for expression of opinion from all sections of the Church. The result of their most faithful and valuable labor was that the new Constitution they reported in 1870 at the Gloucester Convention was adopted, and, submitted to the States, became our working Constitution of to-day in substance.

Our people in the several States are still careless about following scrupulously the General Convention law for uniform procedure. The General Convention rule is that a State Convention shall be composed of all the ordained Universalist clergymen residing in the State and actively engaged in the work of the ministry, unless hindered by sickness; of the officers of the Convention, and of one lay delegate from each parish, and an additional lay delegate for each ——— families contributing to parish expenses. It appears that the different States interpret this rule very freely, and fill in the blank space, referring to the number of families that shall be required to entitle a parish to an extra delegate, in very different ways. In 1897 Rev. John Coleman Adams, D.D., reported for a Committee on relation of State and National Conventions, that the States had in many instances disregarded the General Convention law on this point, and had organized themselves in a number of ways, and had never been disfellowshipped therefor by the General Convention. Some States admitted to their Convention four lay delegates, — two from the society, one from the Church, and one from the Sunday-school. Other States made trustees of schools within their borders, delegates from Associations, delegates from the Y. P. C. U., etc., members of their State Conventions. There is great variety still in actual practice. At this same session of the General Convention, 1897, Rev. F. A. Bisbee, Eben Alexander, and Rev. J. K. Mason, as a committee on the laws of fellowship, reported similar varieties of procedure in the various States regardless of the General Convention law.

Sometimes men refused ordination in one State received it very soon after in another. Ministers disfellowshipped in one State had been restored in another in direct violation of law. The General Convention has not even yet therefore secured uniformity of procedure in all the States in those matters in which such uniformity is plainly most desirable.

Every Universalist ought to stand for uniformity of procedure and obedience to Church law on these matters of general concern. But the encouraging fact stands that we have passed from government by Association, through government by States, into government by a General Convention. "Under the Constitution and rules adopted at Gloucester in 1870, our Denomination has been compacted and set forward, uniformity of ecclesiastical procedure prevails to a wide degree, and, what is vastly more important, the General Convention has become a working power for Church extension and missionary service at home and abroad." The only important particulars in which this Constitution of 1870 has been changed are these: a change in our credal basis of fellowship spoken of in another place, a change from annual to biennial sessions of the Conventions, and a change in response to a feeling that our Convention might well be a larger and more popular body than the laws of 1870 made it. To bring about this latter change, in 1899 an amendment to the Constitution was made, enlarging the membership of the General Convention. The composition of that body now is as follows: —

"1. This Convention shall be composed of the Officers of the Convention, the Presidents, Vice-Presidents and Secretaries of the several State Conventions in its fellowship.

"2. Each State Convention shall be entitled to two clerical and four lay delegates; or having an aggregate of twenty-five parishes and clergymen to two clerical and four lay delegates, and for every additional ten parishes and clergymen to one clerical and two lay delegates. If there be organized Universalist Parishes in any State or Territory which has no Convention they may unite to choose two delegates, and if there be but one such Parish it shall likewise be entitled to two delegates."

This new rule makes it possible that the Convention have 489 delegates, whereas formerly it could have but 216. The first session of the Convention held under the new rule was at Buffalo, in 1901, with 284 delegates present.

The officers of the General Convention are: President, Hon. Frank P. Bennett of Saugus, Mass.; Vice-President, Dr. David Ingalls, Detroit, Mich.; Secretary, Rev. G. L. Demarest, D.D., Manchester, N.H.; Treasurer, Frank W. Wise, Boston.

Trustees: Rev. H. W. Rugg, D.D., Rev. G. L. Perin, D.D., Hon. Eugene F. Endicott, Rev. M. D. Shutter, D.D., Rev. C. Ellwood Nash, D.D., Rev. J. Coleman Adams, D.D., Hon. Charles S. Fobes, F. A. Winkelman, Rev. Almon Gunnison, D.D., Hon. Charles L. Hutchinson, and Rev. G. L. Demarest, D.D., Secretary of the Board. This Board of Trustees is the ruling body in our Church between the biennial sessions of the General Convention.

We do not mean to speak lightly of the value of Associations if they are held as popular gatherings of our people, who may suggest legislation to their State bodies and to the General

Convention, but which surrender all direct ecclesiastical power. The facts seem to indicate, however, that we do not succeed in maintaining much popular interest in religious gatherings shorn of their ecclesiastical power. The Associations have steadily fallen off in attendance since they surrendered governing power to the State. Many of them have entirely died.

After the session of the General Convention became biennial, an attempt was made to hold Conferences in the intervening years. Every attempt was made to provide strong programs and secure special speakers, but the Conferences failed to attract enough of our people to warrant their continuation.

Rev. Q. H. Shinn, D.D., with his splendid missionary enthusiasm, organized in 1881 the Universalist National Summer Meeting. This meeting was held each summer for sixteen years at Weirs, N.H., for three years at Saratoga, N.Y., and for three years at Ferry Beach Park in Maine. At this latter point it holds its 23d annual session in 1904. Rev. Charles E. Lund of Deering, Me., is secretary. The summer meetings at Good Luck and at Rome City, Ind., are further examples of meetings that have possibilities of great usefulness. The old Associations and the Summer Meetings ought to be continued and be made into inspiring mass meetings for our Church.

CHAPTER XII.

THE UNIVERSALIST CREEDS.

SHALL we have a long creed, a short creed, or no creed at all? A long creed is definite, even to details, but its fault is that it cites too many details, and so becomes a source of contention on non-essential matters. A short creed can only give principles, and ought to give only essential principles.

As what seems essential to some, seems unimportant to others, it has always been difficult to make a short creed which gave general satisfaction. Our fathers in the Universalist Church tried for a little time to have no creed at all. They soon found, however, that it would be of great use if there was some short statement that all Churches accepted which could be put into the hands of inquirers as to what Universalists believed. The few Churches that we had from 1780 to 1786 watched with intense interest the lawsuit that Mr. Murray and the Gloucester parish carried on in the Massachusetts courts as to whether the Universalists were a distinct body with power to ordain a minister so that he could legally marry couples. The question was also involved as to whether Universalists must pay taxes to support the Orthodox Church of the town, their own organization not being reckoned to be a Church at all by many.

Then at this time there were two distinct parties at least among the Universalists themselves. There were the Murray school and the Winchester school of Universalists.

As we have before said, the Murray school were Rellyans, while the Winchester school held to some future punishment as necessary to discipline and reform the sinner, Mr. Winchester himself saying that that punishment might be as long as fifty thousand years. There was a strong desire expressed in many quarters that some authoritative statement of what Universalists really believed be issued. It is probable that before the session of the Philadelphia Convention in 1790 a committee had been chosen to draft a creed for that body to act upon.

We do not know who this committee was, nor even that it existed at all; but we do know that Dr. Benjamin Rush of Philadelphia, perhaps our wisest and most influential layman of his day, had a creed put into his hands to put into final shape for committal to the Convention for its action.

This, our first official creed, adopted in May, 1790, is given here in full: —

"SECT. 1. Of the HOLY SCRIPTURES. — We believe the Scriptures of the Old and New Testaments to contain a revelation of the perfections and will of God, and the rule of faith and practice.

"SECT. 2. Of the SUPREME BEING. — We believe in One God, infinite in all his perfections; and that these perfections are all modifications of infinite, adorable, incomprehensible and unchangeable Love.

"SECT. 3. Of the MEDIATOR. — We believe that there is one Mediator between God and men, the man Christ Jesus, in whom dwelleth all the fulness of the Godhead bodily; who, by giving himself a ransom for all, hath redeemed them to God by his blood; and who, by the merit of his death, and the efficacy of his Spirit, will finally restore the whole human race to happiness.

"SECT. 4. Of the HOLY GHOST. — We believe in the Holy Ghost, whose office it is to make known to sinners the truth of their salvation, through the medium of the Holy Scriptures, and to reconcile the hearts of the children of men to God, and thereby dispose them to genuine holiness.

"SECT. 5. Of GOOD WORKS. — We believe in the obligation of the moral law, as the rule of life; and we hold that the love of God manifest to man in a Redeemer, is the best means of producing obedience to that law, and promoting a holy, active, and useful life."

This Convention also made a plan of Church government which was of much use in those early years in unifying our organizations, although the progress was very slow in that direction.

In regard to the debate over this creed in the Convention, we can only judge by the long time occupied in the work, from May 25 to June 8, and from the variety of opinions that we know were represented there. But that there was generous concession and a real Christian desire to promote unity, we know from what was said about this creed in a pamphlet issued at the time. It said: —

> "The articles are few, but they contain the essentials of the Gospel. We thought it improper to require an assent to opinions that are merely speculative, or to introduce *words*, in expressing the articles of our belief, which have been the cause of unchristian controversies."

It is not easy even to-day to improve on that description of what a creed ought to be. Dr. Eddy thinks that there is a Trinitarian intent in these Articles of Faith, although it was stated so mildly that in some quarters the creed was criticised as a denial of the Deity of Christ. The matters of rites, of baptism, of ordinances, etc., were left to individual consciences, and the differences between the Rellyan theology and the Winchester seem to be blended in a statement that both sides accept.

This was our "official" creed for thirteen years, although during that time some of the Churches, notably the one at Boston, amended it beyond recognition. The brethren kept their debating faculties sharpened in criticising this creed, and many believed that a better one could be made. In 1802 a committee of five was chosen to draft a new creed. This committee consisted of Zebulon Streeter, George Richards, Hosea Ballou, Walter Ferriss, and Zephaniah Lathe.

In 1803 the Convention of the New England States, as it was then, met at Winchester, N.H., and among other matters of business was the report of the committee on a new creed, chosen the previous year. Walter Ferriss presented the report, and it is generally supposed that he was the principal author of the creed offered in that report, as he says that he had had no opportunity during the year to meet the rest of the committee. That creed was: —

"ARTICLE I. We believe that the Holy Scriptures of the Old and New Testaments contain a revelation of the character of God and of the duty, interest and final destination of mankind.

"ARTICLE II. We believe that there is one God, whose nature is Love, revealed in one Lord Jesus Christ, by one Holy Spirit of Grace, who will finally restore the whole family of mankind to holiness and happiness.

"ARTICLE III. We believe that holiness and true happiness are inseparably connected, and that believers ought to be careful to maintain order and practise good works; for these things are good and profitable unto men."

The record gives us no account of the debate,

if there was any, over this report. It says that the report was "Deliberately read, naturally considered, and seriously investigated." One account says that the articles were adopted unanimously, but another record says that two voted against them. The Convention consisted of eighteen or twenty ministers and twenty-two laymen, representing thirty-eight societies.

Whatever the rest thought, the clerk who kept the records had a beautiful unconsciousness that they were making and he recording important denominational history.

It is a strange fact that Hosea Ballou made no suggestion as to this creed either at the time or afterward. It evidently had no importance whatever in his eyes. John Murray did not attend the Convention of 1803, and so had no part in making the creed. Nathaniel Stacy was a visitor to the Convention from New York State, and he kept a diary, and afterwards published an Autobiography. Mr. Stacy says that Noah Murray likened the proposed creed to a calf before its horns have appeared. "But it will soon grow older," he said, "and then it will begin to hook." Zephaniah Lathe replied, "All that Brother Murray has offered would be correct had he not made a mistake in the animal. It is not a calf; it is a dove; and whoever heard of a dove having horns at any age?"

The reader can easily see that Mr. Ferriss followed closely the Philadelphia creed in making these Articles of Faith, and that he greatly improved upon his copy.

It has always been a tradition among us that the chief impelling motive to creed-making in 1803 was that we might escape paying taxes to the Orthodox Churches in New England by having a creed of our own to prove that we ourselves were a Church. Dr. Eddy believes that this tradition among us has no ground, and that the only desire was to have some definite Church organization of our parishes and people, with no thought of escaping taxation.

This creed has always been known among us as the Winchester Profession of Faith, and it has always held a very important place in our work. In 1903, exactly one hundred years after the making of this Profession, a notable meeting was held in the historic old church edifice at Winchester. Dr. Cantwell read a most interesting paper, of great historic value, giving the history of that gathering in 1803, and an analysis of their work. We have made free use of that paper here. Dr. Pullman and Dr. Atwood and many others gave valuable addresses, and the great gathering took much delight in honoring the fathers who made for their day so noble a statement of faith. All these addresses and papers, with much more interesting

The Universalist Creeds. 107

matter, are published in the volume referred to in the Introduction to this book.

The Winchester Confession remained our only official statement of belief until 1899, although for twenty-five years preceding that date few Conventions passed without attack and defence of that historic, to many people sacred, document.

As one reads the debates in the records of those years from 1878 to 1899, the old fear that disturbed Noah Murray comes to mind, and it seems that the calf's horns were getting well grown.

The chief grounds of criticism of the Winchester Confession are these: The word "restore" implies a fall from some previous superior condition, generally from a perfect state in Adam, and that the race is to be put back in some condition in which it formerly was that it has lost for a time. Another objection was made that its statement of the connection of holiness and happiness was utilitarianism. Many were the committees chosen, many the cunning rhetoricians who volunteered to make a better creed than this Winchester Confession. The Convention records for the period indicated contain many interesting attempts at creed improvement, all of which attempts were riddled by the adroit critics before they were fairly off the table. At last the Church grew very weary of a discussion that appeared to have outlived its usefulness, and a sigh of relief went up when the Convention of 1899 at Boston adopted the following amendment to the Constitution, proposed at Chicago two years before: —

"I. The Profession of Belief adopted at the session at Winchester, N.H., A.D. 1803, is as follows:

"ARTICLE I. We believe that the Holy Scriptures of the Old and New Testaments contain a revelation of the character of God and of. the duty, interest and final destination of mankind.

"ARTICLE II. We believe that there is one God, whose nature is Love, revealed in one Lord Jesus Christ, by one Holy Spirit of Grace, who will finally restore the whole family of mankind to holiness and happiness.

"ARTICLE III. We believe that holiness and true happiness are inseparably connected, and that believers ought to be careful to maintain order and practise good works; for these things are good and profitable unto men.

"II. The conditions of fellowship shall be as follows:

"1. The acceptance of the essential principles of the Universalist Faith, to wit: 1. The Universal Fatherhood of God; 2. The Spiritual authority and leadership of His Son, Jesus Christ; 3. The trustworthiness of the Bible as containing a revelation from God; 4. The certainty of just retribution for sin; 5. The final harmony of all souls with God.

" The Winchester Profession is commended as containing these principles, but neither this nor any other precise form of words is required as a condition of fellowship, provided always that the principles above stated be professed.

"2. The acknowledgment of the authority of the General Convention and assent to its laws."

This disposition of the creed question seems to be generally satisfactory.

Some have objected to the word "retribution" in the new statement as a word connoting revenge or anger, and others have wished that a belief in the Holy Spirit had been stated as one of our principles. However, those who like the Winchester Confession have perfect liberty to use it; those who object to its wording have entire liberty to state its principles in better words. This action seems to justify our claim to be a Liberal Church. We stand on principles, and not on any fixed form of words.

The most interesting effort that has yet been made to take advantage of this liberty to state the principles of the creed in one's own words, is Dr. Capen's effort to cast the principles of our faith in a form having liturgical value. In the New Gloria the Winchester Profession stands for those who desire to use its time-honored form, and beside it stands this new form for those who prefer it: —

"I believe in God: the Father, Almighty and Universal; and in Jesus Christ his Son, the true teacher, example, and Saviour of the world. I believe in the Holy Spirit, the quickener and comforter of men. I believe in the Holy Scriptures of the Old and New Testaments as a revelation of righteousness and love.

I believe in the Holy Church Universal; in the communion of saints; in the certainty of punishment for transgression; in the forgiveness of sins; in the life immortal; in the final triumph of goodness and mercy; and in the union and harmony at last of all souls with God."

CHAPTER XIII.

UNIVERSALISTS AND MISSIONARY WORK.

If asked to name the characteristics which distinguish a genuine Christian from others, there is one which must be put very near the first. The genuine Christian is fully possessed by the missionary spirit. If he has not this spirit, he is not a Christian, whatever he may profess. Of course the Christian is one who believes Christ, but the only evidence that one believes Christ is that one does what Christ said. "Go ye into all the world," is the Magna Charta of Christianity. "When saw we thee sick and in prison, and visited thee? Inasmuch as ye did it unto the least of these, ye did it unto me." This is Jesus' test of a Christian. The Christian believes some good news; he cannot rest until everybody believes the same good news. No literature is of more thrilling interest than the stories of Christian Missions. How few of our young people have discovered that the best novel is insipid beside the life of Paton in the New Hebrides, or Judson or Cary in India. We ought to have a live Mission

Circle in every parish, reading the lives of the great missionaries, and our own book, "Our Word and Work for Missions." Some one has said that Universalism cuts the nerve of missionary enterprise. There is a certain counterfeit of Universalism, which makes a man a lazy optimist, comforting himself with the notion that God will bring us all through some way, and that we need not worry. But the real Universalist knows that he must help God save the world. The Church has never had any more successful missionaries than Origen, Theodore, and the Gregories, and we think that those men believed the Universalist idea. True, no man will be a missionary who does not believe that men are lost; but is it necessary to believe that they are endlessly lost, if they die an hour before the missionary gets to them? Surely no man could bear that weight and live. Men are lost, that is, they do not know their way, — they are not yet found, — until the saving truth reaches them; and that fact is the spur to all missionary enterprise, be it Universalist or any other.

In comparing the missionary work of the Universalist Church with that of any other, one fact ought always to be remembered. We have not only had to contend against all the difficulties that others meet, such as the sin and spiritual inertia of men; but we have had beside a constant and often a bitter opposition from other denominations of Christians. In the face of this opposition, the fact that we are alive at all proves that we have been heroic missionaries. Murray and Winchester and Ballou and their coadjutors were noble missionaries. As early as 1794 the Convention "chose Elders Michael Coffin and Joab Young to go forth in a circuitous manner and preach the everlasting Gospel." This they faithfully did, probably at their own charges, and most of our preachers have often gone with them on the same terms.

At the session of the Convention at Swanzey, N.H., in 1801, it was "Resolved, that a fund be raised by such ways and means as may hereafter be devised; the amount of such fund is to supply the wants of Brothers sent forth to preach, and to aid in the printing of useful books, and to answer all such charitable purposes as the Convention may judge proper." This is the first attempt of the Convention to raise a missionary fund, and they chose David Ballou, oldest brother of Hosea, as treasurer. His duties could not have been arduous, as he reports to the next session of the Convention that no response whatever had been made to the appeal for a fund. The objections to this fund-raising make curious reading. They are, "First, we remonstrate against banking money for defraying travelling expenses; second, we see something in the plan that looks like ecclesiastical revenue; third, by raising a pretty good sum of money we might get some additional laborers, but we are strongly suspicious of their faithfulness." The Convention met these formidable objections, and renewed its plea for funds, and in 1803 the treasurer reported that he had received $32.03½. The Convention, however, with commendable faith, annually went through the motions of electing a treasurer until 1824, when that needless formality was discontinued.

This feeble effort does not mean that those Universalists had no missionary spirit, it means that they did not know nor care very much about the Convention. The General Convention has always been too far off from individual Universalists to awaken any thrill in them. This apathy still exists, and is the reason why we need personal superintendency. Let us not forget that the attempt to educate our people to give for missions through the General Convention was never seriously made until 1866. At that date the Convention first became incorporated so that it could receive funds. Then, instead of passing a resolution, they sent a live man, Rev. D. C. Tomlinson, to canvass the State of New York for a fund for missionary work of the General Convention. Within a year he raised $17,000, but no other State was canvassed. Since Mr. Tomlinson made this canvass in 1866, the Universalist people have contributed generous sums for missionary work.

The General Convention in 1904 has funds amounting to about $360,000. The various State Conventions have funds aggregating in round numbers $450,000. Beside this, our people have acquired more than ten millions of dollars worth of local church and parish property, and we have more than four millions invested in our schools.

It has already been said that 1870 was observed as the centennial anniversary of the landing of John Murray at Good Luck, N.J. For several years preceding this date, there was much thought as to how this anniversary might be made a most notable occasion.

In 1868, at the session of the Convention in Providence, a special committee was chosen, known as the Centenary Committee, to consider all ways and means to make the Centenary year the greatest year we had yet seen. This committee was A. A. Miner, John D. W. Joy, Richard Frothingham, I. Washburn, Jr., L. W. Ballou, J. G. Bartholomew, D. C. Tomlinson, H. F. Miller, J. S. Cantwell, J. Smith Dodge, Jr., with Richard Eddy as Secretary. In 1869 Dr. Ryder's name was added to this list. At the Buffalo Convention in 1869 this Centenary Committee made its report. It was a Church paper that rose to the occasion, as if we had had a Pope, and this had been his Encyclical letter.

This report called upon all our people first of all to make the Centenary year a year for deep personal searching of conscience and religious quickening. Then it called upon all parishes to make a supreme effort to pay all parish debts of all sorts, and to build new churches, and add to and beautify church property. Then it made a noble plea for remembering all our schools and colleges. Last of all, this report asked that $200,000 be raised as a special memorial fund, to be known forever as the Murray Centenary Fund.

The Rochester parish was asked to give its pastor, Rev. Asa Saxe, D.D., a leave of absence, that he might go into the field and take charge of raising this fund. Rochester responded right loyally, and Dr. Saxe marshalled the hosts and organized the task.

All State Conventions were summoned to help, men were put into the field to canvass the separate States where possible, and plans were made for great mass meetings in the large centres of population. Twenty-five thousand missionary boxes were made, and more than twelve thousand of these boxes were put into the homes of our people. The missionary box was suggested to Rev. E. G. Brooks, when he was Secretary of the Convention in 1867, by D. L.

Holden, Esq., of New Jersey, and in 1868 the Providence session of the Convention approved the plan. Later Mr. Holden became Treasurer of the Convention, and Dr. J. M. Pullman Secretary, and they made the missionary box idea for a time very successful.

So in 1870 the great Centenary Convention met at Gloucester, where John Murray had his first parish in America. It was the largest gathering of Universalists that the world has yet seen. The meetings were held in a great tent seating thousands of people, and overflow meetings were held in all the churches in the town. Dr. Miner preached a Centenary Occasional Sermon. Dr. Chapin preached the Sermon before Communion. Horace Greeley and John R. Buchtel, and P. T. Barnum and Governor Perham, and scores of men and women whose names are mentioned in these pages as builders of our institutions, were there, all joining in plans to enlarge the borders of our Church. Dr. Saxe made his report of the great year's work. Our people had given $948,537 as their Centennial offering. This included all sums given for schools, debts, new buildings, and the Murray Fund. It included all we had given that year outside of parish running expenses. Every other gift to our Church was counted except the usual gifts for ordinary parish expenses. The Murray Fund itself was reported as having reached in cash and good pledges the total of $135,000. This Murray Fund stands to-day as $142,958.03; and the income from it is used in the aid of theological education, the distribution of Universalist literature, Church extension, and the missionary cause.

The significance of this fund is not more in its amount than in the fact that the raising of it was the first thing that the whole Universalist Church in all the world ever tried to do all together. It was the first glimpse that we ever had of what we might do if we would only all lift together at the same object, under the direction of the central governing body.

In 1882 Rev. Thomas B. Thayer, D.D., made a stirring address before the Massachusetts Convention on Foreign Missions, which awakened much interest. That same year the Trustees of the General Convention in their seventeenth annual report — note that it was only the seventeenth — said, "The time has come for the Universalist Church to look toward the establishment of missions in heathen lands." In 1883 the Trustees again urged this matter. These utterances were the first expressions of what many individuals were thinking about.

The call of the world's mission fields was beginning to pierce the ears of Universalists. The Church was getting ready to attempt its next task as one whole united body. In 1886, when

Universalists and Missionary Work. 119

the Convention was twenty years old, it appointed as a special committee, to consider the whole matter of foreign missions, Rev. H. W. Rugg, D.D., Rev. E. H. Capen, D.D., Rev. Asa Saxe, D.D., Hon. Olney Arnold, and Mr. A. T. Foster. This committee began a most systematic study of the whole situation.

Rev. J. H. Chapin, D.D., of Meriden, Conn., went to Japan, in part as an agent of the Convention, to study that country as a field for our Church to enter. The Committee reported in 1887 that in their judgment the time was ripe for the Universalist Church to enter the foreign missionary field, and that Japan offered the most favorable opportunity for such work.

The Convention heartily adopted the report of the committee, and the canvass for funds began. The Sunday-school at Stamford, Conn., has the honor of having made the first contribution for the Japan Mission, followed very closely by the Young People's Missionary Association of the Church of the Messiah at Philadelphia. The Trustees of the Convention now appointed Dr. Rugg, Dr. Sweetser, and Dr. Demarest the standing committee on foreign missions; and in 1889 this committee invited Rev. G. L. Perin, D.D., of Boston to undertake the work of missionary to Japan.

Dr. Perin accepted the task to which he was thus called by the enthusiastic voice of the whole Church, and early in January, 1890, entered upon an energetic canvass to increase the $21,000 already pledged for the Mission to $30,000, the sum supposed to be required for five years.

Dr. Rugg joined with Dr. Perin and the editor of the "Leader" in making one issue of the Church paper a "Japan Paper," and the last Sunday in January, 1890, was the first "Japan Sunday."

Dr. Perin's spirited canvass soon increased the fund to $60,000, and this was an epoch in the Universalist Church the most notable since the Centenary year.

In the spring of 1890, Dr. Perin, the first Universalist Missionary of modern times, landed in Japan. Mr. I. Wallace Cate and Miss Margaret C. Schouler accompanied Dr. Perin as his assistants. In 1892 Rev. C. E. Rice went to Japan to add further strength to the little company of Universalists there. In 1893 Miss Schouler, acting under her physician's advice, returned to America. The Church remembers with honor her first woman in the foreign mission field. For a time Mrs. I. W. Cate had charge of the Girls' School left by Miss Schouler.

In 1894 a contract was renewed with Mr. Cate for further five years' service, and Rev. Edgar Leavitt was sent out from America to re-enforce the workers in Japan. That same

Universalists and Missionary Work. 121

year Dr. Perin resigned and returned to America. In 1895 Miss Catherine M. Osborn went to take her place in the Japan Mission force, and, with the exception of a very brief recess in 1900, Miss Osborn has served her Master and her Church continuously ever since in the Japan work. In 1897 Rev. Mr. Cate requested to be released from further service in the foreign field, and returned home. Mr. Rice, the President of the work in Japan, was now left with only Mr. Leavitt and Miss Osborn as American helpers. Early in the year 1899 Mr. Rice retired from the Japan work after nearly seven years of very successful labor.

In 1899 Rev. G. I. Keirn took Mr. Rice's place as superintendent of the Japan Mission, remaining in the field and working with notable success until late in 1901, when the illness of Mrs. Keirn made it necessary for him to resign. In 1901 Rev. Wallace Cate sailed for Japan for the second time, after having given already seven years to this service. Mr. Cate is still in the field, and deserves our honor and hearty support and loving sympathy for his work with this mission. In 1904 Miss Claudia E. Schrock was selected by the Woman's Centenary Association to go out and assist in the increasing labors of the Japan Mission, and is now in the field.

We have five ordained native Japanese ministers who render invaluable service in the work These are Rev. Hidezo Yoshimura, — who visited this country in 1897, impressing very favorably our people who had the privilege of meeting him, — Rev. Hisanari Hoshino, Rev. S. Akashi, Rev. Sempo Ito, and Rev. Kyoshi Satoh. Miss Tame Imai, a Japanese young lady, and Mr. Satoh just mentioned, have been in the United States and have studied at Lombard and Tufts College. Miss Imai was in the care of the Women's Universalist Missionary Society of Massachusetts, and greatly interested all our people who knew her. Mr. Satoh was ordained in the Every Day Church in Boston in 1903, and has returned to the work in his native land. Miss Imai has also been a most welcome addition to the teaching force in Japan. A new church edifice was erected in Tokyo in 1903, and the Blackmer Girls' Home was also opened in that year. This home is named after Mr. Lucius Blackmer of St. Louis, whose generous thoughtfulness and wisdom made the Home possible. All these workers, men and women alike, have well earned the lasting gratitude and honor of our whole Church. Let them never be out of mind because they are out of sight.

This chapter must speak a word of Home Missions, although the list of those who have sacrificed here, — often sacrificed as much as any worker in foreign fields, — is so long that

Universalists and Missionary Work. 123

some will be forgotten in an attempt to tell the story. The General Convention, aided by the State bodies, has set workers in the field at Washington, Albany, Schenectady, Omaha, Lincoln, Oakland, Pasadena, Riverside, Cleveland, Denver, and Spokane. The workers in some of these fields have left no marked result, yet often the toil has been heroic.

In nearly all the fields, as in Denver and Spokane, beautiful church edifices have risen, and permanent results achieved. It often means men and women of finest talents working on the frontier far from all Universalist fellowship, often weary and alone. All honor to the Universalist missionaries, from Halifax to Tokyo, from Hico and Pensacola to St. Paul and Spokane. Let us not forget our faithful missionaries. Pray for them daily. Help them.

Our ministers and laymen will yet need long training before we come to our full measure of strength as missionaries. Let every home, every parish, every pulpit, every Sunday-school, be a training-place for the true missionary spirit until we are able to send laborers into every whitening field to gather the rich harvests awaiting us there.

As the twentieth century came in, we set our

NOTE. — The work of Rev. James Billings and Rev. Mary C. Billings in Texas, for many years has been of great use and is very precious to remember.

faces toward the third great task that we have ever tried to do all together. This was the raising of the Twentieth Century Fund for Missions. The sum was fixed at $100,000; and Dr. Perin again took the field, and with him toiled many in all the States, and in a few months the sum was subscribed. This fund was raised on pledges running for three annual payments, and at this writing $76,133.42 has been actually paid in, in cash.

Let us awaken to a sense of our power. We are a Denomination; and when every one lifts at the same time at the same task, in the same spirit of consecrated devotion, we shall surprise ourselves at the magnitude of the tasks we can perform.

CHAPTER XIV.

SUNDAY-SCHOOLS AND CHILDREN.

FROM the very beginning of their organized work, Universalists have thought much about proper training for children. Indeed, our Church stands among the very earliest pioneers of the Sunday-school movement in America. Prof. Austin Phelps says that his father, pastor of a Congregational parish in Brookfield, Mass., in 1816, heard of a Sunday-school in America, and the next day organized one in his own parish. Many of his people thought that such an institution desecrated the Sabbath, but the young pastor insisted.

This Sunday-school that Mr. Phelps heard of as existing in 1816 might have been one of our own, as there was a distinctively Universalist organization by that name in the Lombard Street Church in Philadelphia as early as that date.

Twenty-six years earlier than this, however, in 1790, Dr. Benjamin Rush, a strong Universalist, founded a non-sectarian organization in Philadelphia known as the "First Day or Sunday-school Society."

That same year, 1790, Dr. Rush prepared a very strong series of resolutions on the religious instruction of children for the Philadelphia Convention of Universalists, which were heartily adopted.

In 1791 Mr. Oliver Dean, a deacon in John Murray's church in Boston, opened a school like this one of Dr. Rush's.

But in 1816 we got to an organized Universalist Sunday-school, and few, if any, were earlier in this country. Dr. Eddy says that the second Sunday-school was opened by Rev. Paul Dean in Boston in 1817, and the third in Gloucester in 1820. So we were in the field of Sunday-school work with the very first to enter it in America, and the idea has steadily grown with us and spread through all our churches. Few indeed are the Conventions and Associations that have not studied ways and means to strengthen this department of our work. Many of our older pastors prepared excellent helps, service books, catechisms, and lessons for Sunday-school work. Shippie Townsend prepared a Universalist catechism as early as 1787, and many have followed his example since.

In 1865 the Rhode Island Convention caused a catechism to be prepared which has been very widely used among us, known as the Rhode Island Catechism. Dr. John Coleman Adams's Universalist Catechism published in the "Helper"

Sunday-schools and Children. 127

is of great value. One could almost fill these pages with lists of service books and song books, prepared by Universalists and published for Sunday-schools. Dr. Bartholomew, Dr. Demarest, Dr. Fletcher, and many others referred to elsewhere, have prepared liturgies and service books that have had wide and lasting influence. For many years the General Convention kept a special Committee on Sunday-schools, and their annual reports were a feature of the Conventions.

In 1870 Samuel A. Briggs began the publication in Chicago of the "Universalist Helper" for Sunday-schools. Then this publication was moved to New York, and prepared for one year by Rev. George W. Perry. Since then it has been printed in Boston, and has been edited by Dr. Demarest, Rev. J. G. Adams, D.D., and to-day is prepared each month by Rev. Oscar F. Safford, D.D., as editor-in-chief. Dr. Safford's work for Universalist Sunday-schools is of the greatest value. Maizie Blaikie Barney is in charge of the Primary Department of the "Helper," and her work is also very useful. It would be impossible to print even the names of all those who have helped, with skilful pen, these editors to make the "Helper." The result of all that work has been to make the "Universalist Helper" a standard Sunday-school magazine.

In 1883 a Sunday-school Library Commission was appointed, to recommend books suitable for such libraries, and to prepare and publish from time to time lists of such books. This Commission is still continued, and renders conspicuous aid in its department of the work.

In 1886, under the auspices of the General Convention, a Sunday-school Superintendents' Bureau of Exchange was established. Mr. W. H. Hart, the accomplished superintendent of the Sunday-school of the Church of the Messiah in Philadelphia, and others, put much toil and study into this Bureau. As one reads the reports made, and the ideals of results held, one wonders that so useful an institution as this Bureau was ever given up. But the reports that began in 1886 were given annually only four years, and then the Bureau ceased to be.

In the year 1888 the question as to the usefulness of the International Lessons was raised among us, and the discussions and studies that have grown out of that question are of great use. A Commission, consisting of J. Coleman Adams, C. Ellwood Nash, F. O. Hall, H. B. Metcalf, and E. F. Pember made an elaborate and careful report of the whole matter to the Convention in 1889. This Commission thought that the International Lesson system was far better than any method that had preceded it, and in the exposition of these lessons provided

Sunday-schools and Children.   129

by the industry and genius of Dr. Pullman they thought that our Church had a help for teachers equal to any known. The Commission made a careful estimate of the two plans, one to use the International Lessons, the other some special series prepared by our own theologians, and concluded their report by saying that the "Commission had no recommendation to make." They saw that any change must grow, and not be made off hand.

The matter did not occupy the attention of the General Convention again for ten years; but in the mean time it was discussed at State Conventions, Associations, Sunday-school Institutes, and through the Press. In 1899 the Trustees of the General Convention invited Rev. G. A. Kratzer to come before them. They had been requested by the Western New York Sunday-school Institute to do this, and they asked Mr. Kratzer to explain fully what his associates wished to have done and how to do it. The result was that another Commission of five was chosen, consisting of J. Coleman Adams, G. A. Kratzer, C. Ellwood Nash, Prof. Arthur W. Pierce, and Miss Maizie Blaikie, to take the whole matter into consideration, and report at the next session of the General Convention. This report is a very valuable summary of the whole matter of our Sunday-school work.

The Commission found that many, perhaps a

majority, approved the International Lessons; but there were a large number who wanted something else. The Commission therefore recommended that our Sunday-schools be graded into five departments, as follows: I. The Kindergarten Department, including all children under 7. II. The Primary Department, children from 7 to 10. III. The Junior Department, children from 10 to 13. IV. The Middle Department, children from 13 to 15. V. The Senior Department. For the Junior and Middle Departments the Commission recommended the International Lessons with some supervision; but for the other Departments specially prepared lessons.

In 1901 the Commission reported again, Mr. E. F. Endicott having been substituted for Miss Blaikie, in other respects the members of the Commission remaining as before. This Commission recommended for the Kindergarten Department the lessons prepared by Mrs. Maizie Blaikie Barney; for Primary grades, the lessons on the Life of Jesus written by Mrs. Marion I. Noyes; for Junior grades, two series of lessons, the one on "Cardinal Virtues," and the other on "Topical Studies in the Teaching of Jesus," both prepared by Dr. Nash; for Intermediate and Senior grades, Dr. Pullman's Studies in Paul and the Life of Jesus, and a series of lessons from the Old Testament treated from the modern view-point, by Rev. F. W. Perkins. The work on Bible Study by Rev. J. B. Smith was emphatically recommended by this Commission also. The final recommendation of his Commission was that increased attention to Sunday-school work be given by all State Conventions, Summer Meetings, Associations and similar gatherings.

The Publishing House has made the utmost possible efforts to serve the Church according to these expressed desires. It publishes the International Lessons, with most excellent exposition and comment for teachers, for those schools that prefer them, and it also is now publishing a new course of lessons edited by Rev. D. M. Hodge, Rev. F. W. Perkins, and Rev. J. F. Thompson. These last-named lessons are published in Manuals, each containing thirteen undated lessons, at fifteen cents a copy. The work of these manuals so far has been on "The Kingdom of God in Israel," the first quarter on "The Making of the Nation," and the second on "The Times of the Judges." We are promised very soon two more Manuals on the "Life and Teachings of Jesus." These lessons are based on the best modern knowledge of the Bible, and we have no better denominational expression of the way the Church reads the Bible to-day in what we have called the third stage of our theology.

Here in clear, brief form, the student can see the growth from John Murray's thought of the Book, and Hosea Ballou's thought of it, to the modern thought of it. Any Sunday-school can begin the use of these Manuals at any time, and elect for itself the time which it will spend on each Testament. The Commission on Sunday-schools at present is composed of Rev. J. C. Adams, D.D., Chairman, Rev. G. A. Kratzer, Secretary, Mrs. Maizie Blaikie Barney, Prof. A. W. Pierce, Rev. C. Ellwood Nash, D.D., and Hon. E. F. Endicott. So between the "Helper" and the Manuals and the suggestions of the Commission and the readiness of the Publishing House to aid, if there is anywhere in our Church a poor Sunday-school it must be because of some local failure to take advantage of these helps.

What a noble list of names of great Sunday-school superintendents our Church has on its rolls! Whittemore, Goddard, Joy, Carpenter, Hart, Hutchinson, Metcalf, and Cole are names which stir most beautiful memories and associations in hosts of souls. This is only the beginning of the list of those who everywhere have rendered invaluable service to their Church in this field of Sunday-school work. What an inviting field for consecrated men and women this work is! One can only wonder that more do not seek it. One could scarcely exaggerate

Sunday-schools and Children. 133

the possibilities of eternal good open in every parish in our denomination to young men who will enter this work. Even a man of moderate talents may by study, consecration, and earnest preparation, fill a place as superintendent of a Sunday-school or as a teacher there, which any minister may well envy.

In regard to the relation of children to the Church in other ways than through the Sunday-school, we have many interesting examples. There are two ideas in regard to this relation. One idea is the Catholic idea, that every child born is born into the Church as truly as it is into the home, and that fact should be at once recognized by baptism of the infant. The other idea has been that no one could come into the Church until mature enough to understand the step. Very nearly all Universalists to-day believe that children should be baptized in infancy into the Church of Christ, and when they are mature enough should by public confirmation accept the act done for them in infancy as their own.

When John Murray was in Gloucester as pastor he was often urged by parents to baptize and christen their children. He could not conscientiously give infants baptism, since he held that the New Testament taught that only believers could be baptized. But it seemed very clear to Mr. Murray that the children were

God's children, and that nothing could be more appropriate than a public ceremony recognizing that great fact. So about the year 1780 he began to hold services of Dedication of Children. This beautiful service attracted many among us by its fitness. Dr. Eddy quotes an incident, as told by Rev. S. R. Smith, that will interest young people, as it relates to Father Stacy, one of our most loved and revered pioneer ministers, and tells how he dedicated a child of Mr. and Mrs. Thurlow Weed, then of Albany. This was in 1819, in Norwich, N.Y., in a Baptist church our people were using for a special service. "At the conclusion of these services, Rev. Mr. Stacy placed himself at the altar, and announced that the rite of dedication was to be administered. The parents came forward and presented the infant, when the administrator offered a short prayer. There was the hush and stillness of death over the congregation, for, as few had ever witnessed the rite, every one seemed intent on seeing and hearing everything connected with its administration. Immediately after the prayer, Mr. Stacy took the child in his arms, and commenced the benediction; but after uttering a few words his voice sunk — he paused — the service was wholly suspended. Yet no one moved; moments, minutes even passed; still all seemed fixed in their places and in silence. I ventured to look over the pulpit in which I was standing. Beneath it stood the good man, tenderly holding the child in his arms, his face turned toward the heavens, the tears streaming down his cheeks, and his utterance denied by the overwhelming intensity of his feelings. Soon the whole congregation burst into tears, and sighs and sobs spoke forth the deep emotions of the heart. The service was resumed and suitably closed, and that congregation broke up with deeper and more hallowed feelings than ordinarily falls to the lot of worshippers. For there was a beauty and propriety in the service which owned God as Father; which acknowledged his right to give and to take away; and which sought his blessing upon the head of infant innocence, that soothed and won and satisfied the soul."

In June, 1856, Rev. C. H. Leonard, D. D., then pastor of the Church in Chelsea, instituted Children's Sunday. The interest in the custom steadily grew, until in 1867 it came before the General Convention sitting in Baltimore. A committee, of which Rev. L. J. Fletcher was chairman, offered resolutions that "As a first act looking to a Christian life, to the upbuilding of the cause of Universalism, and to the glory of God as an end, the little child should be dedicated to the care and service of Almighty God at the earliest convenient time, and from that moment be educated for and brought into the Sunday-school, and then still onward into the Christian Church." This was followed by a strong recommendation that the names of all children thus dedicated be entered in the records of the Church, and that they should be considered candidates for Church-membership as soon as they reached a suitable age.

In 1868 the Convention by formal vote set apart the second Sunday in June of each year as Children's Sunday.

As far as is known, this observation of Children's Day is everywhere accepted by us. We have added to the ceremony of Dedication the rite of baptism very generally, and the confession of faith and the reception into the Church of Christ follow when the child comes to suitable age. We are still very far from making of this service all we might and ought. Every Universalist ought personally to know every child that has been dedicated in his local church during his connection with that church. He ought to be the guardian, friend and grown-up protector of that child. This feeling of deep responsibility for children, especially for the children of our own Church, would save many a life at its most critical period. How many of us there are that witness the christening and baptism of children in our church on Children's

Day, and never give the matter another thought! There is no magic power in rites. That rite is useful which awakens conscience and impresses duty. Let us care for the children of the Universalist Church

CHAPTER XV.

THE YOUNG PEOPLE'S CHRISTIAN UNION.

The reasons which led to the organization of the young people in the Universalist Church were precisely the same reasons which have impelled all other denominations to the same step.

However well the Sunday-school does its work, there is a gap between it and the Church organization when the youth feels too old for the former and no vital interest in the latter. To pilot young people safely across this perilous gap, Rev. F. E. Clark, pastor of a Congregational church in Portland, Me., organized in 1881 a Young People's Society of Christian Endeavor. This Y. P. S. C. E. is perhaps the most notable religious movement of the last fifty years. It has gone round the world, and from the very first our own young people were interested in it.

There had been young people's societies of various kinds in many of our parishes for years preceding this; but these societies had been for local purposes, social or literary. Much is to be said, however, in favor of these early societies, and every parish ought to be a busy centre of the social and literary work for young people. The first feeling that found expression among us about amalgamating these isolated local societies, was that they might be more distinctly allied with denominational missionary work.

We have spoken of the raising of the Murray Centenary Fund, and of the important place the missionary box played in that notable movement. The first enthusiasm over these boxes had somewhat abated after a few years, and the committee was trying to find some way to make them effective again. Mrs. George B. Marsh, who was a most useful member of the Board of Trustees of the General Convention for ten years, and the only woman who was ever on that Board, formulated a plan in 1885 to organize in all our churches Young People's Missionary Associations. This plan was adopted by the Convention in 1886; and a model Constitution was prepared, and a copy of it, with a very urgent explanatory letter, was sent to all our parishes.

So the Y. P. M. A. — the first effort the Universalist Church made to combine all its scattered local young people's societies under one name and for one purpose — was born, and started on its way. Much hard work, much thought and prayer, went into this first effort to organize all our young people; but the movement, nevertheless, failed to win any widespread or enthusiastic response. Many faithful workers were sorely disappointed that the Y. P. M. A. did not spring into popularity. "Father" Clark's Endeavor Societies were sweeping round the world, and many were asking why our own young people did not respond to the call of their Church. But the "wind bloweth where it listeth," and the Y. P. M. A. had no notable place among us.

We never had more than sixty-three of these Associations. Let us not think, however, that all these efforts to organize our young people, first into social and literary, and then into missionary, societies were failures. In these ways God was leading us, and we were finding that interest in missions could not precede but must always follow personal religious culture and love for the Master. The records of those years show plainly that our young people were more and more attracted by the Christian Endeavor idea.

Between 1881 and 1889 we had thirty-eight Y. P. S. C. E. Societies. During those same years· about twenty-two other societies were listed in the Register which seemed to exist for religious work, and these, with the sixty-three Y. P. M. A. named above, made about one hundred and twenty-three young people's societies of the religious sort. It is not easy to tell when and where the movement began to combine all these into a more distinctively religious movement than before. The truth is, that the time for that change was ripe everywhere, the hour had struck, many in Israel were looking for it.

In 1883 Rev. S. H. Roblin was in Victor, N.Y., the writer of this book was in Rochester, Rev. Mr. Leland was in the vicinity, and James Tillinghast was a young lawyer in Buffalo. Together these workers were publishing a little Church paper, which they had named the "Universalist Union." This was the name of a paper which Rev. W. S. Balch and O. A. Skinner had published back in the forties, but the young editors were not thinking so much of that as they were of promoting union of their own young people in the Church they were set to build. They were full of plans for the young people, and at least one of them had made a beginning toward a Y. P. S. C. E. in his parish. Mr. Roblin soon moved to Bay City, Mich., and he organized a Y. P. S. C. E. there that had some most excellent material in it. From this Bay City Society there went out, on Feb. 22, 1889, an open letter to all young people's societies known, of whatsoever name, proposing that an attempt be made to get together and form a national union of some sort. In the East the same feeling was growing that we have noted in western New York and in Bay City.

There was a very earnest young people's society in Lynn, Mass., and the General Convention of 1889 was appointed to meet in Lynn that year. These young people of the Lynn parish sought and easily obtained permission to call a meeting of all the young people's societies of our Church at Lynn on the day preceding the Convention session. The Lynn parish sent out a most generous invitation far and wide for the young people to come up and consult together about a national organization.

Although already heavily taxed to entertain the great General Convention, they gladly assumed all the extra burden this young people's call involved. The call to come to Lynn in 1889 went out, and they did come. Some were there who did not quite know whether they could slip in with the boys and girls undetected, and pass as young people, or not; some were there who have since grown too old for the young people's society, as every one ought to do in proper season; some were there who have since found the land of eternal youth; but no one who was there will ever forget the thrill and joy of it, and it almost seemed to us as if we were witnessing the birth of a New Universalist Church. The young people of the land sent up to Lynn that year 131 delegates representing 56 young people's societies from 13 States, and they held their first meeting Oct. 22, 1889.

Young People's Christian Union. 143

After a brief meeting of praise and prayer, the task of organizing was begun. The name, National Young People's Christian Union of the Universalist Church, was adopted. In later years when Canada and Japan were heard from, the Union became known as the Central Union,[1] and the society is always known as the Y. P. C. U.

The Constitution, adopted the next day, stated the object of the organization to be "To promote an earnest Christian life among the young people of the Universalist Church, and the sympathetic union of all young people's societies in their efforts to make themselves more useful in the service of God."

The motto of the Y. P. C. U. is, "For Christ and his Church," and its watchword is "Onward." The Union has always been most heartily loyal to the General Convention, and never for a moment have the relations of cordial helpfulness between them been strained.

At this first Lynn Convention, Lee E. Joslyn — a Bay City boy, as was most fitting — was chosen President, James D. Tillinghast of Buffalo was made Secretary, Nannie Jenison of Lynn Treasurer. The Executive Board consisted of J. Thomas Moore of Philadelphia, Clara B. Adams of Lynn, Angie M. Brooks of Portland, and Belle Gibson of Chicago.

---

[1] The Union is incorporated, however, under the name of National Y. P. C. U.

The little western New York paper referred to above, the "Universalist Union," was made the organ of the Y. P. C. U., and the full report of this Lynn meeting was printed in it, and 2,500 copies were distributed throughout the land. This paper was published for years by Secretary Tillinghast as the Y. P. C. U. paper, largely on his own responsibility; but in 1893 the Union took entire control of the paper, and the Universalist Publishing House issued it, dividing profit or loss with the Central Union. The name of the paper was changed to "Onward," which name it still bears. It is still published by the Publishing House, but is now managed by the Central Union. Its editors, since Mr. Tillinghast, have been Rev. Omer G. Petrie, Rev. Harry L. Canfield assisted by Mary Grace Canfield, Rev. E. G. Mason, Grace F. White, and Charles Neal Barney. The present editor is Secretary Harry Adams Hersey, and under his management "Onward" is being issued in a new form, and greatly improved, and put thoroughly in touch with every department of Y. P. C. U. work. It costs fifty cents a year, and every one interested in the coming Universalist Church should study every number.

The first regular Convention of the Y. P. C. U. was in Rochester, N.Y., Oct. 20 and 21, 1890. Later it became evident that the Union could do its work better and have more time if it held its annual meetings apart from the sessions of the General Convention; so in 1894 the Union Convention met in July, and it has continued to meet in that month ever since.

These July annual meetings of the Y. P. C. U. have been very notable assemblies. No gatherings of our Church equal them in importance except the biennial sessions of the General Convention; and compared even with these great meetings, the Y. P. C. U. Conventions do not suffer in numbers, in splendid enthusiasm, in efficient capable leadership, in excellent business methods, nor in missionary results.

The Boston Convention in 1895 taxed to the utmost of seating and standing capacity two large churches.

In Lynn the tenth annual Convention in 1899 was made a special decennial jubilee of the Union, in the city of its birth. The Lynn depot, and many of the stores, factories, and homes, were profusely decorated with bunting in blue and white, the Y. P. C. U. colors; and as the delegations from the various States came into the great church, waving State banners and singing State songs, it made the pulses thrill. Soon the large church was full, and a neighboring Congregational church was opened for an overflow meeting. Dr. Pullman's opening words in his address of welcome have stayed in our hearts since: —

"And what is Universalism? It is belief in a capable God, who does not let his worlds run away with him; an adequate God, who is equal to the solution of his problem, and is able to conduct his universe to the good he aims at without the intervention of an eternal catastrophe: therefore all evil is vulnerable, and every soul is saveable."

The Convention at Portland, Me., in 1902, was pronounced by one Universalist at least to have been the finest gathering ever held under Universalist auspices.

The Convention at Akron, in 1903, was not as large as some have been, but it gave the most cheering business reports that any Convention had heard; and the young people have their thought on Providence, and the meeting of 1904, determined that it shall be fully up to the high standard of Y. P. C. U. Conventions.

Mr. Lee E. Joslyn held the office of President until 1892, when Mr. Herbert B. Briggs was elected. In 1894 Rev. Elmer J. Felt succeeded Mr. Briggs, and in 1897 was himself succeeded by Mr. Harry M. Fowler. Mr. Fowler was President until 1900, when Mr. Louis Annin Ames came to the Chair, and he still occupies it. Mr. Ames fills this very responsible office in a way that puts our whole denomination under deep and lasting obligation to him. He administers the office with tireless attention to details, is a model presiding officer, and the hearts of the young people beat as one heart under his magnetic leadership.

Mr. Tillinghast was Secretary of the Union through all its formative years from 1889 to 1894. He is now a useful clergyman in our Church, and his work all those years as Secretary and editor gives him a warm place in the affections of all Unioners of those days. Rev. Harry L. Canfield, who became Secretary in 1894, holding the office until 1898, was a tireless worker for the Y. P. C. U., and not a little of its strength has come from the shaping skill of Mr. Canfield's heart and brain. Rev. Alfred J. Cardall was Secretary from 1898 until 1901, and then Rev. C. Neal Barney held the office for two years. These two also filled the rather thankless but very important office of Secretary with much strength and consecration. In 1903 Mr. Harry Adams Hersey came to this work, and no one has ever done it better than he is doing it.

Miss Nannie Jenison, the first Treasurer, held that office until 1892, when it went to Miss Lizzie Goldthwaite, then in 1895 to Mr. Harry M. Fowler, and to Rev. Omer G. Petrie in 1897, and to Mr. Louis Annin Ames in 1889; and no dollar has ever been mislaid or unaccounted for in the history of this office. In 1890 Mr. George

F. Sears came to the Treasurer's office, which he still holds, much to the satisfaction of all.

The Y. P. C. U. started its missionary career in most energetic, even audacious fashion, before it was fairly a year old; and when those whose hearts were in the older Y. P. M. A. saw what it was doing, they soon transferred their allegiance to the new organization.

The National, or, as we call it now, the Central Union, was incorporated so that it could hold property or receive bequests, at first under the laws of the State of Massachusetts in 1893; but on March 10, 1898, it was reincorporated under its present form. At the first Regular Convention, that in Rochester in 1890, the Y. P. C. U. accepted the offer of the East Tennessee Land Company of two lots of land in Harriman, Tenn., on condition that a church be erected thereon within two years. The Union promptly met the condition, and in 1891 had Rev. W. H. McGlauflin, D.D., in the Harriman field; and in 1894 the Y. P. C. U. went down to Harriman and held its fifth annual Convention in the first church its hands had built, of course not forgetting the generous local support. The city of Harriman has had its reverses, and the parish has seen very trying years; but it has already paid all it cost in the two young people it has given to our ministry, and in the light that has gone from it through all the South.

Dr. McGlauflin, under the direction of the Union, next moved on to Atlanta. A lot was secured there, and a church was built, and in 1900 the Y. P. C. U. Convention held its eleventh annual session in the Atlanta church, the second product of its missionary zeal. Early in 1904 Dr. McGlauflin felt constrained to accept the call of the General Convention to the Northwestern field, and to resign the Southern field in which he had toiled with such notable ability and success. Rev. Clarence J. Harris was called to be Dr. McGlauflin's successor at Atlanta. "It is interesting to note," writes Secretary Hersey, "that Mr. Harris was formerly a Baptist minister, and was converted to Universalism by Dr. McGlauflin in the Atlanta church. Mr. Harris is the fourth minister who has come into our denomination through the Atlanta church."

Since 1901 the Union has given assistance to the Little Rock, Ark., parish. The Little Rock Society is small, and the work encounters much resistance there; but the few are loyal, and respond to the Union's efforts, and they keep open doors, and have a substantial sum of money toward a new church edifice.

"The St. Paul Society is backed solely by the Y. P. C. U.," says President Ames, "and is the most promising field of missionary work we have yet undertaken. We already have a good stone chapel there, valued at $10,000, and a beautiful new church is virtually assured."

The contributions of the young people for all these missionary enterprises are collected through the now famous two-cents-a-week plan. A set of fifty-two envelopes is given to every one who will receive it, in one of which envelopes two cents are deposited each week. This money is forwarded to headquarters, and from there goes direct to the mission field, all expenses of collection being paid from another source. Since 1895 the contributions from this source alone have been $15,925.21.

In recent years several thoughtful persons have given the Central Union twenty-six dollars toward a permanent Fund known as the Permanent Two-cents-a-week Fund. It will be seen that the interest on this twenty-six dollars amounts to two cents a week, and so one goes on giving his payment to the Y. P. C. U. work as long as money draws interest. This Fund now amounts to $295.25. The contributions to missions increased 33 per cent in 1903, and they are still increasing.

In 1894, at the Harriman Convention, the Union added to its work a Junior Union Department. This most important line of work was put in the charge of Mrs. Mary Grace Canfield for development, and with great devotion and skill she fostered the movement. Mrs. Canfield is one of the many who has given years of unselfish service to the Union work.

In 1898 Mrs. Canfield prepared and issued a Junior Star Song Book for her little folks to use. The first thousand copies paid for the cost, and since then about a thousand copies annually are sold. Mrs. Canfield gives all the little book earns above actual cost to the Y. P. C. U. missionary work. The Star Song Book has earned enough to put a $150 window in the Atlanta church, and to give the same church $100 toward its organ fund. There is at present enough money for a window in the next church the Y. P. C. U. may build, perhaps at Little Rock; and this window is to be a memorial for the Canfields' little son Murray, gone from their home.

Since 1898 Miss Lilian Hosley has been Superintendent of the Junior Unions, and she is managing them with great efficiency and consecrated devotion. The Juniors are reaching out their hands in many kinds of service for Christ and his Church. Among other things they have had a hand in the education of little Suye, a Japanese girl.

We have room only to mention by name the other departments of Y. P. C. U. work, beside that of Missions and of Junior work. The Post Office Mission has sent thousands of pages of Universalist literature all over the South, and the world indeed, with many results that give keenest satisfaction. The Good Citizenship Department is another very valuable field to cultivate, and has attracted to us helpers from many denominations. Information about these Departments, and about "Onward," and all details of Y. P. C. U. work, can always be had from the Secretary, whose permanent headquarters are at 30 West Street, Boston.

Perhaps fully as important as any work named, after all, is the work that the Y. P. C. U. has done and is doing in all the local parishes where it has branches. The devotional meetings, the social gatherings, the flower missions, the religious culture, and personal expression of religious life, — of these works there is no human record, and yet we know that they are very great.

One rather unique kind of work the Central Union has done is to get Rev. Almon Gunnison, D.D., to prepare a lecture on "The Universalist Church of To-day," and illustrate it with many lantern-slides of our prominent leaders and Church edifices. This lecture is loaned to the parishes that desire it, and it is in constant demand.

Miss Grace F. White has done many useful tasks for the Y. P. C. U., and among them she has prepared two singing-books called "Praise and Thanks," which are widely used in the service of song at the devotional meetings of the Unions.

Young People's Christian Union. 153

Miss Clara Adams has written a very useful History of the Y. P. C. U., covering the first ten years of its work, from which many facts given here are taken.

It is to be devoutly hoped that every parish in the denomination will have a Y. P. C. U. with all its departments active, and that every young Universalist will be an active member, that this youngest of our great organizations may go on to ever-increasing service "For Christ and His Church."

We must keep it a *young* people's organization. Let its older members move on into the adult department of Church work, and let the young people have this work. Trust them to learn wisdom by having responsibility put upon them, just as we all have to learn it. The Y. P. C. U. must move on, on broad lines. Beware of narrowness. Those who have no gift in audible prayer or public address, and so who sit silent in the devotional meetings, may have some other gifts equally useful in God's great vineyard. Set every young person at work in some branch of Christ's service where he can cultivate the gift that is in him.

The old Literary Society had its uses, the Y. P. M. A. had its uses. Hold fast all the good of the past, and move on broad lines toward the future. The Holy Spirit makes some to speak with tongues, and some to interpret, and some for everything that God wants done for man. Shall not the National Y. P. C. U. be broad and liberal and wise enough to use all the gifts of the Spirit in all sorts of young people?

Although the Y. P. C. U. of the Universalist Church is only fifteen years old, it has its list of those who have passed on, touched by the sacrament of death. Some of these names shall stand on these pages in loving remembrance. Rev. Omer G. Petrie died in 1900 after several years of valuable service in Union work. Rev. Harry Veazie, a son of the Harriman Church, and Miss Ellen F. Calhoun were drowned by the overturning of a boat on a lake at Greensboro, Vt., in 1899. Many will recall with great joy the words and works of these young disciples. Another name of precious memory is Annie H. Stevens, who gave herself in loving devotion to her Church, dying in 1900. A fragrant, a singularly beautiful memory among us is Lucy Sibley McGlauflin. She was a most gifted and consecrated worker beside her husband, Dr. McGlauflin, at Rochester, Minn., and Harriman, Tenn., and Atlanta, Ga., where she died in 1898. Every one will add many names to this list. We love and cherish the memory of all who have died in the work. May their mantles fall on us, the living!

CHAPTER XVI.

THE UNIVERSALIST CHURCH AND EDUCATION.

DR. SAWYER, in the occasional sermon at Akron, O., in 1843, lamented with eloquent tongue, that we had no theological schools, and that so many of our preachers leaped from anvil to pulpit with no technical training whatever. His lament was not new, as the matter of theological training had been debated since 1814 in our Conventions, and many committees had been chosen to study the matter. In 1815 Rev. Paul Dean visited the Western Association in the State of New York, to lay before the brethren plans for a theological school to be established in Massachusetts. Rev. N. Stacy, who was the most influential man in the Association at that time, frankly told Mr. Dean that he should oppose his project, and so it was not presented. Mr. Stacy's reasons for opposing theological schools make good food for thought. They were these: "I would establish a literary institution for the education of young men, but I would have them go alone to the school of Christ — to the Holy Bible — to obtain their divinity, and not to human theological institutions." Every one who has had anything to do with theological schools must often have wished that the young men in them had taken a more thorough course in Nathaniel Stacy's divinity department. Mr. Stacy also objected to the gratuitous instruction of young men, saying that it laid a temptation before idle and unprincipled youngsters to make a profession for the sake of getting an education, and acquiring a living without labor. It has generally been understood that Hosea Ballou felt about as Father Stacy did, and for the same reasons.

So for a long time we had no theological schools. Hosea Ballou 2d met a class of young men in his study, and a study with Hosea Ballou 2d in the chair was a School not to be lightly spoken of. Dr. J. S. Lee had a theological class at South Woodstock in 1856–57, preparing nine young men for the ministry. Dr. Clowes and Stephen R. Smith trained thirty-seven young men for the ministry at Clinton, N.Y. Dr. Sawyer was a mighty talker, but he was also a doer of the word; and in 1845 he surrendered the pastorate of the Orchard Street Church in New York, — a Church which he made so famous that its name has passed into a proverb among us for stalwart preaching and intelligent believing, — and launched into untried work, and uncertain pay, as Principal of Clin-

The Church and Education. 157

ton Liberal Institute. He planned to devote two hours each day to a class of students for the ministry. This arrangement continued about seven years, and Dr. Sawyer trained thirty-seven ministers during that time. Richard Eddy, C. H. Leonard, C. A. Skinner, D. C. Tomlinson, and J. H. Tuttle were in that school, and so it was a great school.

This old Clinton Liberal Institute where Dr. Sawyer did his first notable work as a teacher, and where so many others worked, met with a fate that is a source of regret to many of its old students. In 1879 the famous old School moved to Fort Plain, N.Y. In 1900 its beautiful and expensive buildings there were burned, and the trustees and friends thought it best to move what remained of the property to Canton, N.Y., to continue the educational work of our Church, for which all its funds were given, in connection with St. Lawrence University.

About 1852-53 the New York Universalist Education Society was formed, to advance the work begun at Clinton, and establish a Theological School. In 1853 Rev. Eben Frances, and later Rev. J. T. Goodrich, went into that hardest of all tasks, the task of canvassing for money to put the dream of a Theological School into visible form. Mr. Jacob Harsen of the old Bleecker Street Church in New York gave $5,000, and a little later pledged one thousand dollars to every five thousand given by other parties. This pledge made the Theological School possible. Canton, N.Y., was chosen for the site, and in 1856 a building was dedicated at that place, and the first Universalist Theological School since the days of Origen was begun. Ebenezer Fisher was chosen President of this school, and in 1858 he accepted the position and began the work. Dr. Fisher held this position twenty-one years, dying in 1879 in his classroom surrounded by his pupils. Perhaps one-third of the ministers in our Church at the time of Dr. Fisher's death had been under his instruction. An excellent Biography of Dr. Fisher was prepared by his friend and fellow-worker Dr. Emerson. Dr. Atwood was the successor of Dr. Fisher, coming to Canton in 1879, and serving until he was called to be the General Superintendent of our Church in 1899. Rev. Almon Gunnison, D.D., is now the President.

The Divinity Department of Tufts College was established in 1869, thus making that our second Theological School in order of time. This School of the Prophets was made possible by the noble gift of Sylvanus Packard, one of our great laymen. In 1869 Dr. Sawyer in the height of his splendid power and fame came to this School, and from the very start made it great. Here he remained until his death in 1899, the last years being the honored Professor Emeritus.

Here Dr. Leonard now is Dean, and is rounding out a long life of notable service for our Church.

Our third Theological School in order of time is the Ryder Divinity School in connection with Lombard College at Galesburg, Ill. It is named after the Rev. W. H. Ryder, D.D., of deathless fame among us, whose munificent bequest for this School exceeded fifty thousand dollars. Rev. C. Ellwood Nash, D.D., was President until 1904, when he resigned to accept the office of Field Secretary of the General Convention. Nehemiah White is Dean of the Divinity Department.

Our missionaries in Japan have had, almost from the first, a Theological School in Tokyo, to instruct native preachers, and this Seminary has been very useful.

The Universalist Church has four Colleges under its auspices. These are, Tufts College, Massachusetts, — this is also the Post Office name, — St. Lawrence University at Canton, N.Y., with its Law Department in Brooklyn, Lombard College at Galesburg, Ill., and Buchtel College at Akron, O. All special information about these Colleges is easily accessible to any one who will write for it. But our history ought to have a word about the noble men and women who have built these Colleges for our Church, to enable it to do its full share in educating the world.

Mr. Charles Tufts, who, about 1850, gave twenty acres of land lying a few miles out of Boston, and who later increased this gift to more than a hundred acres, is the man whose name is most fitly given to our greatest School. To this College, Hosea Ballou 2d came as first President, being in that office from 1853 until his death in 1861. A College with Dr. Ballou at its head, whatever it may have lacked in other ways in its pioneer days, was from the first a genuine College.

Most of us knew Dr. Miner as Pastor of Columbus Avenue Church in Boston, and he filled that office in a way that made him great among us forever. But beside this, Dr. Miner was the President, the saver, almost the maker of Tufts College from 1862 to 1874. When Dr. Ballou rose in death, Dr. Miner's parish contributed at various times over $536,000 to Tufts; and more than this, they voted to release their pastor from parish duties and let him serve Tufts as President. For the first three and a half years of this arrangement the parish paid his salary; later Dr. Miner had an assistant in the parish work, and his full salary was paid by the College.

In 1874 Dr. Miner resigned the College work, and Dr. Capen, the present head, took it up, and has made the greater Tufts of which our whole Church is proud to-day. The names of

Tufts and Packard, Walker, Dean, Thomas and Mary Goddard, P. T. Barnum, John D. W. Joy, and Miner and Paige and Metcalf, are built into Tufts to-day in enduring stone and more enduring memories.

St. Lawrence University has its handsome Fisher Memorial Hall built in 1883 by the friends and old students of Dr. Fisher. The Library Building bears the name of Silas Herring of New York, and keeps it a living name. The Reading Room Building, given by Mr. E. H. Cole of Brooklyn, is beautiful enough to be a lasting memorial of the Christian character of the builder. St. Lawrence enshrines the names of some of the greatest teachers our Church has produced. Rev. J. S. Lee, D.D., came to Canton in 1859 as President of the College, which position he filled until 1869, when he became a professor in the Theological School. In this he toiled as long as strength permitted, and was then Emeritus Professor, dying full of honors in 1902. One-third of our ministers, including seven Presidents of Colleges, have been under the instruction of this teacher. Rev. A. G. Gaines, D.D., died in Canton early in 1903. His name in Canton is what Arnold's name was at Rugby. He stamped the indelible impress of the strength of his character upon every student who came into St. Lawrence in the days of his power.

Rev. James Henry Chapin is a name Canton loves. Here the quiet Christian scholar came from time to time each year and met his classes, and with many a student he will walk forever in beautiful companionship. Mrs. Chapin has endowed here the Chapin Professorship, a fit monument for a rare and wonderful spirit. The names of Moore, Craig, Hayward, Ryder, Cummings, Dockstader, Taylor, Gage, Bordwell, Richardson, and Cole are built into St. Lawrence. Dr. Fisk, Dr. Hervey, and Dr. John Clarence Lee have served St. Lawrence as Presidents; and to-day Dr. Almon Gunnison has charge of the School, and the work is moving on.

Lombard College has grown out of a school established in Illinois in 1852 named the Illinois Liberal Institute. Here Rev. Paul Kendall and Miss Caroline Woodbury were Principals. In 1853 the Institute was raised to College grade. In 1855 the whole plant burned, but Mr. Benjamin Lombard came to the rescue, making new buildings fairer than the old possible by generous gifts, and the College was named Lombard University in his honor. In 1898 this name was changed to Lombard College by the action of the Trustees. Prof. Parker, the quiet scholar whom only his students know fitly, has been at Lombard as a teacher nearly forty-five years, honored and loved by a throng of men and women. Prof. Standish was for years a strong

The Church and Education. 163

and notable teacher at Lombard, and with him stand the names of Nehemiah White, Otis Skinner, J. P. Weston, William Livingston, and others. Dr. C. Ellwood Nash was the president of Lombard until 1904, and our Church has produced no finer man to be a teacher and inspirer of youth. Dr. Ryder's name is built into Lombard as it is into Tufts and Canton, and our whole Church; and with him stand Hall, Conger, Throop, Higginbotham, and Waterman.

In 1867 the Ohio Convention began to agitate the question of a College, and in 1870 voted to establish one at Akron if the citizens of Summit County would raise sixty thousand dollars. John R. Buchtel gave more than half this sum, and inspired the raising of the rest of it, and no name is more fitting than Buchtel for the new College. The College opened in 1872 with Rev. S. H. McCollester, D.D., as president, and he was followed by Rev. E. L. Rexford, D.D., and he by Rev. Orello Cone, D.D. This line of strong teachers made Buchtel a vigorous plant, of use and power from the first. Rev. Ira Allen Priest, D.D., came to the Presidency in 1897, and affairs moved on well until on Dec. 20, 1899, the main college building burned to the ground, and a dark hour for Buchtel had come. But President Priest was too strong to be extinguished by any dark hour, and a year had not passed before a new Buchtel Hall was completed, and the College rose out of its baptism of fire fairer than ever. Rev. Augustus B. Church, D.D., is now President of Buchtel, and is launched upon a strong and increasingly successful tide of usefulness for our Ohio College. Crouse and Messenger, Hilton, Pierce, and Mrs. Elizabeth Buchtel, Ainsworth, Dr. Ryder, Isaac and Lovinia Kelly, and William Pitt Curtis, have made gifts for education at Buchtel which will be serving mankind long after the bodies of flesh and the cemetery marbles have gone back to dust.

At different times some fifteen or twenty Academies have been under the control of our Church, but changing conditions have left but three of them to-day. These Academies are Westbrook at Portland, Me., with O. H. Perry as Principal; Dean Academy at Franklin, Mass., with Arthur W. Pierce as principal; and Goddard Seminary at Barre, Vt., with O. K. Hollister as principal. In the days when these schools were planted, there was not an academy in the country where the children of liberal Christians could be free from the tactics of the revivalist and the proselyter. Our fathers built these schools in self-defence. To a large extent that condition has passed away.

Then, when these academies were built, there were large sections of our country where there were no schools of high grade, and these schools were much needed. To-day every village supports its High School, and this fact has made the need of the academy supported by denominational effort somewhat less apparent. Nevertheless, these three Academies named are doing their full share of the work of education of the world.

Dean Academy at Franklin is built on the ground formerly belonging to the estate of Rev. Nathaniel Emmons, the great New England champion of orthodoxy. This fact would undoubtedly have disturbed the good man at one stage of his work, but now we make no doubt that he looks upon it with entire complacency. Dr. Oliver Dean gave the land, and from time to time large sums of money to the institution which now so fitly bears his name. Dr. Dean also gave liberally for Tufts College.

Goddard Seminary bears the name of Thomas and Mary Goddard, already spoken of in connection with Tufts College. Two finer spirits no denomination delights in, nor holds in more precious and beautiful remembrance. At Westbrook, Hersey and McArthur, and Thomas Goddard again, and Sawyer and Miss Niles, have planted a useful institution on enduring foundations.

The reading of even this brief chapter must make it plain to the young Universalist that he belongs to a denomination that loves knowledge and hates ignorance. Considering our numbers, our recent organization for work, the constant theological battles we have had to fight for our faith, we submit our educational record to the world as one that needs no apology. Let us go on with our work for science, knowledge, and popular education.

CHAPTER XVII.

THE WOMEN OF THE UNIVERSALIST CHURCH.

In 1904 Rev. O. F. Safford, D.D., wrote a word of the office and work of the pastor's wife. He was speaking of Mrs. Helen Cushing Dearborn, and she was a perfect example of his thought. "Pastors' wives," said Dr. Safford, "some day, some where, they will receive the recognition they deserve. The unnoted work they have done for Christ shall be recounted."

Not only does the story of the pastors' wives make a story that can never be written; but the story of "Ladies' Aid Societies" of our Church, and the women who have led in them, if it could but once be adequately written, would make a chapter as heroic as any in history. That chapter, however, is written only in heaven; we merely gather a few leaves of it here.

The Universalist Church has had, from a very early period, women enrolled among its ministers. Maria Cook is probably the earliest of these, having received an informal letter of fellowship entitling her to preach, at the Western Association in 1811. Miss Cook seems to have been a woman of ability, and was for some years of service to the Church. She died at Geneva, N.Y., in 1835. Since then we have had a large number of women in our pulpits, and in usefulness they have averaged about the same as an equal number of men taken as they graduate together from our schools.

The Register for 1904 showed about sixty women preachers among us, of whom about one-half are in regular pastoral work. At the same time, it must be admitted that the heads of our Seminaries very seldom receive a letter from any parish asking that a woman minister be sent them. This may arise from the fact that the woman ministry is new and unfamiliar, and the objection may in time pass away. A liberal Church will certainly desire to give every woman the same privilege it gives any man, of self realization and expression in the way the Lord calls.

A notable list is easily made of women who have been advocates of our faith with their pens. Dr. John G. Adams names first in the list Phœbe and Alice Cary, and then goes on to speak of Mrs. Sarah Broughton, Mrs. Julia Scott, Mrs. S. C. E. Mayo, Charlotte Jerauld, Julia A. Carney, Mary A. Livermore, and others. Few young people will recognize these names, but their poems and papers fill large space in the files of our Church papers and magazines.

From 1840 to 1857 an annual named "The Rose of Sharon" was of great service to the Church. Miss Edgarton, named above as Mrs. Mayo as she later was by marriage, edited ten of these annuals, and Mrs. Caroline M. Sawyer the others. The life of Caroline M. Fisher, later Mrs. T. J. Sawyer, is now for the first time given to the world in Dr. Eddy's fine Biography of Dr. and Mrs. Sawyer. Many of Mrs. Sawyer's poems are given in Dr. Eddy's book, and richly deserve preservation.

Beginning in 1851, Mrs. Mary A. Livermore, whose fame is now world-wide, began the issue of an annual entitled "The Lily of the Valley," of which eight volumes were published. Copies of these annuals are still seen in the houses of the older Universalists, and are highly prized.

The "Myrtle," our paper for children, had as associate editors for some years, first Mrs. Phœbe Hanaford, and later Mrs. Bingham. Since 1875 Mrs. E. M. Bruce has been sole editor of this paper.

Mrs. Caroline M. Soule has done considerable editorial work among us, at one time publishing an annual, "The Rose Bud," and later editing a semi-monthly called the "Guiding Star."

For many years Mrs. Jane L. Patterson, beside writing several successful books, was editor of the Home Department of the "Leader." Much of the work that she did in this department is worthy of being preserved in more permanent form.

In Mrs. Hanson's book, "Our Woman Workers," we have accounts of a host of loyal women in our Church.

As we have seen, in one sense, 1870 was the hundredth anniversary of our birth as a Church; in another sense, it was the year of our birth. In that year the amended Constitution fixing the relations of the State Conventions and the General Convention first became active; in that year was the first successful attempt made to enlist our whole Church in one great, notable missionary enterprise. That enterprise was to raise the Murray Centenary Fund, and our women bore a very remarkable part of that work.

At Buffalo in 1869 the feature of the program of the General Convention in session there was to lay plans, and set in motion the machinery, so that at Gloucester it might be reported that a hundred thousand dollars had been raised as a Murray Centenary Fund, the income of which was forever to be used for missionary purposes.

While the deliberations were going on in the auditorium, a company of women gathered in the Sunday-school rooms in the basement of the church-building. They were vitally interested in uniting the whole Church in raising this Murray Fund. None of them had any very definite plans; they only wanted to find out the best way to help. Mrs. D. C. Tomlinson presided, Mrs. Whitcomb was secretary, Mrs. Emma Bailey prayed. The spirit of the Lord came upon them. In due time Mrs. Caroline A. Soule found her way to the stand, and, for the first time in her life she declares, to speak in meeting. Her speech was certainly blessed of God, and the Woman's Centenary Aid Association of the Universalist Church was organized then and there.

Gradually rumors of what the women were doing in the vestry began to reach the audience upstairs, and the effect was inspiring. Mrs. Soule was elected first President of this first Woman's Association of our Church, and as far as possible one Vice-President was chosen from every State. These women went back to their various home States and took up the work of raising the Murray Fund with tireless enthusiasm. They held a series of brilliant meetings in various prominent churches during the year, and in September they came up to the big Centenary Convention at Gloucester to report. Here the Universalist women of America held their first national gathering, filling an auditorium, the vestry below, and two other near-by churches. Mrs. J. G. Adams, the treasurer, reported that they had raised during the year for the Centenary Fund $33,359.38, and that the total expense of the canvass had been $773.73. Mrs. Caroline A. Soule, presiding, introduced Mrs. Bowles and Miss Chapin and Mrs. Livermore, and the addresses made by these women were worthy of the great occasion.

As these lines are being written, word comes across the sea of the death of Mrs. Soule, this first President of the Centenary Association. She died in December, 1903. Mrs. Soule had made her home in Scotland, where she died, these latter years, and her name will not call up any clear picture to many of the young people. But those who know will write Mrs. Soule's name among the very first women of our Church. Mrs. Soule was once Principal of the female department of Clinton Liberal Institute. She was married to Rev. Henry B. Soule in 1843, and was left a widow in 1852. She published a Memoir of Mr. Soule soon after his death. She wrote constantly for our periodicals, and was associate editor of "The Ladies' Repository," editor of "Guiding Star," and of the "Christian Leader" (New York) for seven months.

So when the Centenary women wanted a President, Mrs. Soule was naturally the one they wanted. Her means were very slender; and it is a beautiful deed to remember, that, at the conclusion of Mrs. Livermore's great address at Gloucester in that Centenary meeting, she proposed that five hundred dollars be raised for Mrs. Soule then and there as token of their love and honor. Seldom has that sum of money been found more quickly than it was that day, and never more worthily bestowed.

After the Murray Fund was raised, the special task for which the Association had organized was completed, but it was evident to all that opportunities for permanent work and possibilities of usefulness were simply endless for such a society of women workers as this. So in 1871 at the Convention in Philadelphia, it was voted to continue the Association, striking out the word "Aid" from the name used that first year. So ever since our Church has had among its most useful organizations the Woman's Centenary Association, popularly known as the W. C. A.

Mrs. Soule remained President of this Association until 1880, when she was succeeded by Mrs. M. Louise Thomas. When Mrs. Thomas gave up this task, Mrs. Cordelia Quinby was chosen President. Mrs. Thomas and Mrs. Quinby were the wives of two of our most noted clergymen, and, both being widowed, they took up this work in the Church for which their husbands had toiled so faithfully, and greatly strengthened our cause by their consecrated, skilful toil. Mrs. Quinby now holds the office of Honorary President, Mrs. Zelia E. Harris of Watertown, N.Y., being the acting President.

The W. C. A. has had but three treasurers in the thirty-four years of its existence. The first of these was Mrs. M. A. Adams, who served until 1883, and then Mrs. M. M. Dean, and then the present incumbent, Mrs. T. A. Williams of Washington. The Association is an incorporated body, so it can receive bequests and hold and manage property, and it has to-day a permanent fund of $21,113.70.

No task has ever been undertaken in our Church in which the women have not had a generous hand. Money for these gifts and for the permanent fund comes largely from the annual membership fees of one dollar asked of every member; or from gifts of twenty dollars, making one a life member; or from gifts of one hundred dollars, making one a "patron." Of course, many contributions and special gifts are received outside these regular sources of income.

About twelve years ago the W. C. A. revised its Constitution so as to bring the central body into closer touch with its scattered local constituency. It now holds an Annual Convention, consisting of officers of the National Society, Presidents of unorganized States, Presidents and Secretaries of State Missionary Societies, with delegates from every local Missionary

Circle, one delegate for every nine members being received. Then under this National Convention there are, in as many States as it is possible to secure them, Women's Universalist Missionary Societies for that State, made up of the President and one member from each local Mission Circle. Then each State Society takes measures to organize a Mission Circle in each parish in the State. The National Society sends out to each Mission Circle a program of meetings for a season, giving a course of study of Missions of the greatest value.

In 1902 Mrs. Ella E. Manning, the recording Secretary of the W. C. A., reported that the Association had voted to make their sessions biennial instead of annual, and to hold them at the same time and place of the General Convention. The representation was enlarged so as to include one delegate from every twenty members at large or from any Woman's Auxiliary Society paying the annual dues. While the annual membership fee remains one dollar, thirty-five cents only goes to the national treasury, while sixty-five cents is to be used by the State or Mission Circle. In 1903 the Wisconsin and Minnesota women came to the W. C. A., making twelve State Societies now auxiliary to that Central body.

In the year 1874 the work of establishing a Universalist Church in Glasgow, Scotland, was entered upon by the W. C. A. Universalism was held by a little company in that land of stern theology, and they sent a cry across the sea for help, and the women heard the cry. In 1878 Mrs. Soule went to Scotland, and began a labor lasting four years. How much good her work did, no man knows. At least she found friends, and attached them to her with undying devotion. With some of these friends she made her home in later years, and from that home she died. Rev. J. H. Hanson, D.D., Rev. Marion Crosley, and Rev. C. A. Garst followed Mrs. Soule's four years' pastorate in Glasgow. Scotland has proven a hard soil for organized Universalism; but the seed has been faithfully sowed there obediently to the call of God, and in his time the harvest will surely appear.

In 1886 was organized the Woman's Universalist Missionary Society of Massachusetts, often known as the W. U. M. S. This Society has the same kind of work in hand that the W. C. A. carries on, and is of great use in its State. In 1902, at the Auburn Convention of the W. C. A., the Massachusetts women were received into membership.

The W. U. M. S. among many other good works has taken special interest in caring for women students in Tufts Divinity School. Miss Tame Imai, the young girl from Japan, referred to in another place, has found this Society interested in her welfare, and she goes back to her Japan work with helpful memories of her sisters in America. Nearly all the States that have any organized Universalism, report a woman's society under some name. There is no opposition to each other in these societies, and they are generally in close touch with the W. C. A. Every woman worker in our Church comes to a time, — when it is, she must herself decide, — when she may well ask if it is not better for her to leave the Y. P. C. U. to the Juniors, who are constantly growing ready to enter it, and for her to put her energy henceforth into a Mission Circle under the W. C. A.

Our people, as a rule, are not well instructed in the story of the world's Christian missions. We have no deeper need than that all our parishes, Sunday-schools, homes, be brought into vitalizing, electrifying touch with those heroic men and women who have carried around the world the message of the Christ. There are young men and women who feel drawn toward the ministry, but who do not yet see their way clear to absent themselves from home for the needed study. We suggest to all such the splendid opportunity for ministry in the home Mission Circle and the home Sunday-school. There are few fields open to us that promise such returns as these fields offer to intelligent, consecrated labor. A live Mission Circle, a live

Sunday-school, in every parish in the Universalist denomination, would in a few years revolutionize our Church and multiply its working forces. Try the home ministry. May God bless the noble women of the Universalist Church!

CHAPTER XVIII.

THE UNIVERSALIST PRESS.

DR. EDDY, by diligent research, has discovered one hundred and eighty-two Universalist periodicals published prior to the year 1886. Of all these, only four are published to-day under the same title as is given in Dr. Eddy's list. The four so published are the "Myrtle," the "Sunday School Helper," the "Universalist Herald," and "The Register." All the rest have either disappeared or else been merged in periodicals under another name. If we include in our list of periodicals the local State and parish papers now being published, the list is a long one. It appears that the majority of our preachers have either had some experience in editorial chairs or else are getting some now. Every minister must yearn at times for the privilege of speaking to a larger audience than that which attends his regular Sunday ministrations, and must desire to use the press for that wider hearing. After a time they generally find that the expense and the editorial labor are too much for them, and so the parish paper disappears from one parish to appear in another in endless procession.

In many churches, as in Rochester, N.Y., and in the Church of the Eternal Hope, in New York, the young people bear a large share in the issuing of the paper and mailing it to homes in the parish where they want a message to go. Several State Conventions publish papers to keep the Universalist in touch with State work. This is done very successfully in Illinois and in New York. Some pastors arrange with the regular local papers, paying for a certain amount of space each week, which they keep filled with their parish matters.

About forty years ago the people of our Church, led perhaps largely by Dr. Sawyer and Dr. Miner, began a movement to concentrate all our publishing interests, that we might increase and improve our books and papers. The result of the agitation was, that in 1862 a stock company was organized, and two hundred and fifty shares of stock issued. This stock was quickly taken, most of it by members of Dr. Miner's own parish, and the New England Publishing House was incorporated. In 1867 the name was changed to the "Universalist Publishing House." One of the very first rules adopted was, that as soon as the business paid expenses and redeemed the stock, the institution should pass into the hands of twenty-one permanent or life trustees, to be administered forever for the benefit of the whole Universalist Church. This was realized in 1871. Thus our Publishing House never existed to make money for private individuals, but the men who took the risks and advanced the funds had the good of the whole Church of Christ in their generous and far-seeing minds.

All profits now go to improve the plant, and there is no institution among us more worthy to be remembered by bequests than our Publishing House. Mrs. Mary Goddard at one time gave the House $10,000, and other gifts bring the assets of the institution up to $195,000.

The Publishing House is at 30 West Street, Boston, and it is always open for any purpose that serves the Universalist Church, and so has become our general headquarters. Here the ministers congregate for their Monday Meeting. Here are headquarters for all the Massachusetts, and many of the National, Universalist organizations. If you want to know anything pertaining to our Church that you cannot find out at home, write to the Publishing House about it. They live *for* the Church, and not *off* of it. Order your books and periodicals of your own Publishing House. Make it strong, and it will make the Church strong.

The first of our periodicals was the "Universal Magazine," edited by Rev. Abel Sargent in 1793–94. Its length of life did not correspond with its great name, as it expired in one brief year. However, it taught at least one of the Universals, — that of the love of God.

In 1819 we find Hosea Ballou editing the "Universalist Magazine," which was our first weekly paper. This paper has had many names and forms, it has absorbed others and been absorbed by others, but has come through all these confusing changes, and is now our great Church paper, the "Universalist Leader." It has been named at different times the "Trumpet," the "Universalist," the "Christian Leader." It has absorbed from time to time the "Ambassador," once printed in New York; the "New Covenant," once printed in Chicago; the "Star in the West," once printed in Cincinnati; and the "Gospel Banner," once printed in Augusta, Me.

All these papers, under the present policy of centralization, are united in the "Universalist Leader," printed by the Publishing House at Boston. This paper is now edited by Rev. F. A. Bisbee, D.D., and is managed with great ability for the service of the whole Universalist Church. The "Leader" is indispensable, but its usefulness might be indefinitely multiplied if its circulation could be increased. There must be literally thousands of Universalists who never see it; how, then, can they be served by it?

The Universalist Press.

Every week it has a most vital message for fifty thousand Universalists, but perhaps hardly a tenth part of that number hear the message. How can we act in strong unison without some organ of communication, and how can there be an organ of communication with all unless all connect themselves with the "Leader"?

A bequest of fifty dollars, at interest, will send the "Leader" to somebody, long after the giver is dead. Two dollars a year puts any one in touch with the inspiring message and the plans of our Church for a forward movement.

As one passes his eye over the names of those who have managed our denominational press at divers times, he feels that it is a goodly company of able workers that has toiled here. The two Ballous, Thomas Whittemore, the Streeters, Sylvanus Cobb, G. W. Quinby, A. B. Grosh, W. A. Drew, the Skinners, Dr. Hanson, Dr. Sawyer, Dr. Chapin, Dr. I. D. Williamson, and Dr. G. H. Emerson, are some of the leading names of those who have made a strong Universalist Press and passed on.

Speaking of the dead only, the greatest editor our Church has had, with the possible exception of the Ballous and Thomas Whittemore, was Dr. George H. Emerson. In the length of time he served as editor, he surpassed all others, and in the high quality of that service none have surpassed him. Dr. Emerson died in Salem, Mass., in 1898, aged seventy-five years. After several years in the work of a parish pastor, he succeeded Rev. Hosea Ballou, D.D., as editor of the "Universalist Quarterly." In 1862 he became associate editor of the paper then called the "Universalist," with Dr. Sylvanus Cobb; but two years later he became sole editor, and so continued until 1867, when he was invited to New York to be the editor of the "Christian Ambassador," the title being changed to the "Christian Leader." He so continued until 1872, when he returned to Boston to resume charge of the "Universalist," and so remained until his decease, at which time, through absorption with other papers, it was entitled the "Universalist Leader." Thus Dr. Emerson filled out an editorial career of nearly forty years. Meantime, in the midst of a busy life he found time to make books. He wrote "The Life of Ebenezer Fisher," "The Life of Alonzo Ames Miner," "The Doctrine of Probation Examined," and "God and the Bible," among other volumes. His life was one of great usefulness.

Of those living who have served our Church in the editorial capacity, the name of Rev. J. S. Cantwell, D.D., would by common consent be named first. Dr. Cantwell's name appears as editor of the "Star in the West," as early as 1865, and he has been connected with our Press a large portion of the time since. Dr. Cantwell's vigorous editorials, his clear explanations of our theology when it has been assailed, his consistent and thoughtful Christian life giving forth his words of devotion, have made him a light-bearer to many souls.

Dr. Atwood has served for many years in various editorial capacities, always honoring our Church.

The Publishing House now owns and issues four periodicals; viz., the "Universalist Leader," the "Sunday School Helper," the "Myrtle," and the "Universalist Register." "Onward," the official paper of our Y. P. C. U., is now managed and published by the Central Union, though still printed at the Publishing House, where the Editor, and General Secretary of the Central Union, can always be found.

Beside these periodicals, the House publishes and owns the titles and copyrights of one hundred and fifty volumes. The list of these volumes we make no attempt to print in this book, as it can easily be obtained from the Publishing House at any time.

The "Universalist Herald" is published every Saturday by Rev. J. M. Bowers at Canon, Ga.

It may be said in a general way of the Universalist Press, that it has existed to promote our particular denominational thoughts and interests. We have produced few if any books that can be classed as general literature. Our authors have usually written what our House stands to publish, — books that state and defend some phases of our theology, or the life of some leader among us who has defended that theology. If we have had our eyes too closely fixed on one thing to permit us to write general literature, we have at least stated that one thing clearly and defended it vigorously. We have attended strictly to the leaven that is leavening the whole lump.

We have produced a few books that have had a very wide circulation. A little book called "The Law of Kindness," written in 1839 by Rev. George Montgomery, D.D., — who was pastor of our church in Auburn, and later in Rochester, N.Y., for many years, dying in the latter place in 1898 full of honors, — has had perhaps the widest circulation of any book written among us. It was translated into many languages, and under many variations of its original title, and numerous editions of it were printed round the world, and read.

Dr. Chapin's books, "Hours of Communion,' and the "Crown of Thorns," and T. B. Thayer's book, "Over the River," and Dr. Quinby's book "Heaven our Home," are examples of volumes that passed through many editions, and had a very wide reading, regardless of sects.

The Scholar among us who has written books

on theological topics that have recognition from all scholars in his line of study, is Rev. Orello Cone, D.D., of the Canton Theological School. Dr. Cone has written "Gospel Criticism and Historical Christianity," "The Gospel and its Earliest Interpretations," "Paul, the Man, the Missionary, and the Teacher," and "Rich and Poor in the New Testament."

The scope of this volume does not permit any complete list of books written by Universalists. The Publishing House gladly sends such lists to any who inquire. Neither have we room to name the increasing number of books written by authors outside of our organized Church, who nevertheless explicitly hold and clearly teach our faith. Every young Universalist will find profit and delight in Allin's "Universalism Asserted," or in Cox's "Salvator Mundi," and a long list of similar books.[1]

---

[1] Other books beside those mentioned here and elsewhere, which are worthy of attention, are: "The Purpose of God," by Rev. J. Smith Dodge, D.D., one of our strongest theological works; "The Manuals of Faith and Duty," eleven small volumes by different authors on the following topics : " The Fatherhood of God; " " Jesus the Christ ; " " Revelation ; " " Christ in the Life ; " " Salvation ; " " The Birth from Above ; " " The Church ; " " Heaven ; " " Atonement ; " " Prayer." The Publishing House issues numerous valuable tracts. Excellent samples are the following : Doctrinal, "Universalism, What it is, and What it is Good for," by Rev. O. Cone ; " The Victory of Christ," by Rev. J. Smith Dodge, D.D.; "Why I am a Universalist," by Rev. F. A. Bisbee, D.D. ; same title, by P. T. Barnum ; Practical, "The Church for the New Day," by Rev. F. W. Perkins ; " Four Reasons for Attending Church," by Rev. Henry Blanchard, D.D. ; "The Christian Ministry a Business," by Rev. C. H. Leonard, D.D. Other books by those not of our Church, which are Universalist in statement or spirit, are: " The Spiritual Order," by Thomas Erskine ; " The Destiny of Man," by John Fiske ; " The Ascent of Faith," by Amory Bradford.

The greatest long Poem yet written by a Universalist is "Christus Victor" by Henry Nehemiah Dodge. Mr. Dodge has been given an honorary degree by Tufts College in recognition of this poem, and the work has attracted wide and uniformly favorable notice. Some of the lyrical verses scattered throughout this poem are made to sing, and will find a place in our hymn books. Many young people will like to learn these words from Dr. Dodge's book: —

> How strong art thou, great Son of God?
>   Canst thou bid sin's wild tumult cease?
> Canst thou destroy oppression's rod,
>   And lead the nations forth to peace?
>
> Great Son of God, art thou so strong
>   That we may safely cling to thee,
> Assured, though troubles round us throng,
>   Thy triumph we at last shall see?
>
> Canst thou with life's dark evils cope?
>   Dost thou our fears and sorrows know?
> Canst thou fulfil immortal hope,
>   Or must we to some other go?
>
> To whom, to whom, then, shall we turn?
>   Whose hand shall point our homeward way?
> What other friendly beacons burn
>   With light to guide us to the day?

CHAPTER XIX.

HYMN BOOKS AND LITURGIES.

A STUDY of our denominational literature, while it will undoubtedly show that our work has been very largely polemical, will most emphatically disprove a somewhat common notion that we have neglected the personal religious life. While our supreme work has been theological, we have not failed at least in the endeavor to make our people religious and devotional. As books to kindle personal religious life, those named in the last chapter, Thayer's "Over the River," Quinby's "Heaven our Home," Chapin's "Hours of Communion," and his "Crown of Thorns," have been printed again and again, and had wide circulation and reading. It is probably true that we have many homes among us where there is no such thing as stated daily family worship. We may not be sinners above others in that direction, but we are sinners here. Our Sunday-schools, Churches, and Theological Schools suffer, because so many young people have not grown up in homes where there is an atmosphere of prayer and devotion. From the beginning almost of our Church life in America, books of hymns and prayers for the home have been published among us. Charles Hudson, W. S. Balch, Menzies Rayner, Otis Skinner, A. C. Thomas, and John G. Adams did much work to prepare hymns and prayers for home life. In 1843 Otis Skinner prepared a manual especially to promote family worship. In 1877 Dr. Hanson prepared and published "Manna," a book with a home service for every day in the year. This book has had a steady sale ever since, and has been of great service to our homes. In 1894 the writer asked many of our clergymen to prepare a daily service for use in the home, and these were published under the title " Prayers for the Home."

In regard to Catechisms and Liturgies and Hymn Books for the Sunday-school, we have been very fruitful workers. As has been said, the Universalists were among the very first in America to establish Sunday-schools. As early as 1786–87 we have songs and catechisms for Sunday-schools by Shippie Townsend. Few are the years since that our denomination has not published more or less good Sunday-school literature. Catechisms and Manuals and Hymn Books for Sunday-school work, if they were just named, would fill this chapter.

Balch's "Manual" in 1839, Bacon in 1849,

Lombard in 1860, Fletcher's "Manual and Harp" in 1861, J. G. Bartholomew's "Altar" in 1862, Demarest's "Year of Worship" in 1873, and Slade and Holden, and a host of others since, make a most notable contribution to American Sunday-school work in the line of hymn books and liturgies.

As for a liturgical service for the regular worship in our churches, it must be confessed that our people have been and are intensely congregational in this as in other matters. Every Church makes its own ritual; and a clergyman who has to conduct services in many churches, or a layman who worships in many, has to learn a new order in every place. Some have always regretted this variety, and worked for unity and conformity, but still most of our people seem content with leaving the liturgy to the whims and notions of every minister and every parish.

The reader will remember that one matter discussed at the Philadelphia Convention in 1790 was "one uniform method of Divine worship." This question was not settled then, and it has been lying on the table, taken off for frequent discussion, ever since, but always put back on the table, or indefinitely postponed.

It seems to be certain that our people will never surrender their congregational rights; but it also seems that there is a slowly increasing disposition to have a uniform service for all our Churches, which service shall avoid the absolute fixity of the Episcopal Church on the one hand, and the eccentricities of individuals on the other hand.

We ought to have uniformity without rigidity. To this end, Menzies Rayner prepared a liturgy in 1839, but little or nothing came of it.

In 1857 Thomas's "Gospel Liturgy" appeared. This is a good book; and while it was not used in many congregations, it prepared the way by awakening thoughts in many people on uniformity of service.

In 1864 appeared "The Book of Prayer" by Rev. Charles Leonard, D.D., now of Tufts College. While this book, as a whole, has been used in but few of our congregations, it, more than all previous efforts, has been the established liturgy of our Church. The special services, of baptism, admission of members to the Church, communion, marriage, and burial, are very widely used among us.

In 1866 Dr. Thayer and Dr. Fletcher published "Gloria Patri," as a proposed liturgy. This contains morning and evening services for each Sunday in every month for the year, beside services for special occasions. This book has been quite widely used, and is of great value to us.

In the last issue of our hymn book, "Church

Hymn Books and Liturgies. 193

Harmonies," several orders of service were printed and offered to our people, and something is being done by these toward flexible uniformity.

At the Convention session of 1899 at Boston, the demand for a uniform liturgy seemed strong enough to warrant the selection of a committee to take the whole matter into consideration. Rev. Charles R. Tenney was chairman of this committee, and his associates were Rev. E. H. Capen, D.D., Rev. Henry I. Cushman, D.D., Rev. L. B. Fisher, and Rev. A. J. Canfield, D.D.

This committee gave the matter as careful consideration as was possible, and reported at Buffalo in 1901. The report stated that the "Book of Prayer" by Rev. C. H. Leonard, D.D., and the "Gloria Patri" prepared by Rev. L. J. Fletcher, D.D., in collaboration with Rev. T. B. Thayer, D.D., seemed to be the two books most widely used among us. They recommended that the Publishing House be requested to cause a revision of "Gloria Patri" to be prepared by some competent liturgist, and that they issue it, and that all our congregations adopt it; and so it was hoped that we might reach a uniform service.

The Publishing House, always at the service of the Church, arranged with Dr. Capen to prepare the liturgical, and Prof. Leo R. Lewis the musical, revision of the old "Gloria." This was duly accomplished, and in 1903 the Publishing House issued the "Gloria Patri, Revised," which embodies our best efforts toward a liturgy up to the present time.

In 1904 Rev. G. L. Demarest, the Secretary of the General Convention, issued a pamphlet giving a history of the preparation of this liturgy, and urging all our parishes to adopt it for their Sunday worship. What response this work will meet, it is too early to predict.

It seems that we ought to reach a reasonable, flexible, dignified, uniform order of public worship of God in all our congregations. Our young people can do much toward this important matter. We want a liturgy, uniform enough to shut out ignorant and thoughtless whimsical notions about services, and to give us the rich prayers and forms hallowed by the ages. We want our liturgy flexible enough, however, to give reasonable expression to personal and individual feeling, and especially to be true in its statements. Let us not try and sing and pray what we do not believe. The revised "Gloria" is the best thing yet made by us.

In regard to our hymn-book makers, the reader is referred to Dr. Eddy's treatment of the matter in his chapters in Vol. X. of the "American Church History Series." It seems from this chapter that a great deal of our hymn-making has been making Universalist arguments in rime. The hymns that John Murray edited were pervaded with his peculiar Rellyan theology; and the notion that a devotional hymn could be a theological dogma thrown into rime has long been with us, as with most Protestant churches.

In 1791 the claim of Boston to be the source of American culture vindicated itself in this matter of Hymn Books. In that year the Philadelphia Convention set a committee at work on such a book. The Boston portion of the committee thought that a hymn ought to be for praise and devotion, while the rest thought it ought to be a statement of our theology. The result was, that each faction of the committee published its own book according to its own ideas.

In 1785 Silas Ballou, a layman, residing in Richmond, N.H., gave us a book of hymns, many of which he composed himself, and he had the native Ballou gift of argument, and filled his hymns with it.

Rev. Artis Seagrave and Rev. George Richards were among the most gifted of our early hymn-writers, and many of their hymns are worthy of use to-day.

In 1807 the General Convention appointed a committee, of which Rev. Hosea Ballou was chairman, to prepare a new book of hymns. It is not likely that the Convention meant to in-

struct Mr. Ballou to write the hymns for the
new book all himself, but he did write the
larger number of them. Every man has a
weak point in his armor, and Hosea Ballou's
weak point was the notion that he could write
hymns. He had a fatal facility of riming, which
disease is very common indeed, and let him who
never had it cast the first stone.

Hosea Ballou, however, did write two hymns
which are real hymns made to sing. One was
written to be sung at the General Convention,
and begins: —

> "Dear Lord, behold thy servants here,
> From various parts, together meet,
> To tell their labors through the year,
> And lay the harvest at thy feet."

The other one is: —

> "In God's eternity
> There shall a day arise
> When all the race of man shall be
> With Jesus in the skies."

In 1837 Hosea Ballou 2d published a collection of hymns chosen with fine poetic taste
Two of these he wrote himself, and Universalists ought to sing them gladly. One
begins: —

> "Praise ye the Lord around whose throne
> All heaven in ceaseless worship waits,
> Whose glory fills the worlds unknown;
> Praise ye the Lord from Zion's gates."

The other is: —

> "Ye realms below the skies,
>   Your Maker's praises sing;
> Let boundless honors rise
>   To heaven's eternal King.
> O bless his name whose love extends
> Salvation to the world's far ends."

The Adams and Chapin collection of hymns appeared in 1846, and contains many fine selections for public worship. Dr. Chapin's Christmas hymn, one of the finest in the language, was published here: —

> "Hark, hark, with harps of gold
>   What anthem do they sing!
> The radiant clouds have backward rolled,
>   And angels smite the string."

Dr. Adams here gave to the Church for its permanent enrichment the words: —

> "Heaven is here; its hymns of gladness
>   Cheer the true believer's way."

Our latest and best achievement in hymn-book making is the new edition of "Church Harmonies" issued by the Publishing House in 1901, and in this are many hymns written by our own Universalist singers.

"Good Will Songs," prepared by Rev. Stanford Mitchell, the sweet singer of our Zion, assisted by Mrs. Mitchell, has been and is very useful indeed in our prayer-meetings, and in al our public worship.

Intelligent thought about the hymns that we sing, so we can all sing with the spirit and the understanding, ought to be everywhere encouraged.

CHAPTER XX.

THE UNIVERSALIST CHURCH OF TO-DAY.

As far as figures can show, the status of the Universalist Church to-day is about as follows: We have 980 parishes, 54,325 Church members, 55,000 families. We have 264 young people's organizations, with 7,000 members. We have a Universalist General Convention, the ecclesiastical authority of which is recognized by our Churches the world around. The funds of this Convention aggregate $360,000, the income of which is used to extend our borders in all possible ways. Besides this, we have twenty-four State Conventions, and one Provincial Convention in Ontario, nearly all of them with their own funds for their own State work. The aggregate of these State funds exceeds the General Convention property, being about $450,000. We have ten or more State Conferences, these being organizations in States where there are not yet parishes enough to make a Convention. Our thousand parishes own property aggregating ten millions of dollars. The estimated assets of our schools and colleges is more than four millions. These figures show that Universalists have been generous givers of money for their institutions, especially when it is remembered that these sums are our permanent and invested funds, and do not include the annual constant gifts that we make for local worship and for missions, home and foreign.

A notable characteristic of our Church to-day is a disposition to modify its pure congregationalism in the direction of more superintendency. It is true that for thirty years the General Convention has been the head, the co-ordinating authority, of our denomination. But the authority of the General Convention leaves much to be desired in the way of personal leadership. Some one said, "No one ever saw a tear in the eyes of a Committee;" and so the Convention leadership lacks the personal touch. It is better to send a live man than a printed circular. In 1898 Dr. Nash, encouraged by the brethren, issued a word that came to be known among us as the "Chicago Covenant." It took this name as the spirit which it expresses found very emphatic expression at the General Convention in Chicago in 1897. The Covenant is as follows: —

"We, the ordained ministers of the Universalist Church, profoundly desiring to give full proof of our ministry, by making the utmost of our united strength in the upbuilding of the divine kingdom on earth, and in order to promote a deeper unity of purpose among ourselves through the cultivation of a spirit of loyalty and subordination in the practical administration of the Church, hereby mutually covenant with each other, and solemnly pledge to our beloved Church, that we will at all times hold ourselves in due subjection to the authorities and policies of the Universalist Church, to that end subordinating when needful our personal preferences, and that we will earnestly endeavor to sustain the appointed authorities of the Church, and to carry into effect the policies adopted by the Conventions."

This was tacitly understood to be a measure looking toward the appointment of a General Superintendent, whose function should resemble that of a Bishop as far as the temper of our Church permits. Nearly two-thirds of our ministers signed this Covenant. In obedience to this expression, and in accordance with instructions given them by the Chicago Convention of 1897, the Trustees began to look for some one to call to this most important post of General Superintendent. The unanimous choice of the Board was Rev. I. M. Atwood, D.D., President of the Canton Theological School. Dr. Atwood was not quite ready to attempt such a radical experiment unconditionally, so he arranged for a leave of absence from his school for one year, and went into the field to study the situation. In 1898 Dr. Atwood formally resigned his Canton work, and became the General Superintendent of the Universalist Church. The creation of this office of General Superintendent logically implies that we need not only such an officer over the whole Church, but under him a Superintendent of every State, and often District superintendency under State Superintendents.

This system of superintendency we have fairly entered upon, and it is steadily being perfected. Rev. Q. H. Shinn, D.D., is the Southern Missionary or Superintendent, having a general oversight, under Dr. Atwood, of all the Southern States. Rev. W. H. McGlauflin, D.D., is Superintendent, in the same way, over Minnesota, Wisconsin, and Iowa.

The individual States under superintendency seem to be Georgia under Rev. Thomas Chapman, South Carolina under Rev. J. S. Rasnake, Illinois under Rev. J. S. Cook, Indiana under Rev. Marion Crosley, Kansas under Rev. G. A. King, Kentucky under Rev. Arthur Roberts, Maine under Rev. F. E. Barton, Massachusetts under Rev. Charles Conklin, and under him District Missionaries, Missouri under Rev. G. E. Cunningham, New Jersey under Rev. Henry R. Rose, New York under Rev. W. W. Hooper, and under him District Missionaries, Ohio under Rev. O. E. Colegrove, Pennsylvania under Rev. J. D. Tillinghast, and Texas under A. G. Strain. This system of superintendency ought to bring every parish, and almost every individual, in our denomination into close personal touch with the whole Church, and the whole Church into touch with each part.

While we give the name "General Superintendent" to our national office, that does not mean that its incumbent has any governing power. He is the appointee of the Convention Trustees, and not an officer of the Convention. He is appointed by the Board, and subject to their removal for cause, and is not elected from the floor of the Convention. He works strictly under the direction of the Board of Trustees. Our Church is governed by its biennial Conventions, and between the sessions of the Convention by its Board of Trustees. On questions of State policy each State is governed by its Convention, and between sessions by its executive board.

In addition to the strong movement toward superintendency, the General Convention at its session of 1903 created the office of Field Secretary. Rev. C. Ellwood Nash, D.D., was the unanimous choice of the Trustees of the General Convention for this office, and in 1904 he resigned the Presidency of Lombard College and accepted this office of Field Secretary. This office perhaps ought not to be spoken of as a new one, since, under slightly varying terms, it has been known and used by us many times. In 1870 Dr. Saxe took the field to raise the Murray Fund under the name General Secretary. Before that, Rev. E. G. Brooks, D.D., had been employed as General Agent, to raise money and give personal aid to all Church interests. Rev. R. H. Pullman was General Secretary several years about 1874–1876. Rev. C. B. Lynn was Assistant Secretary from 1891–1894. Rev. H. W. Rugg, D.D., was Financial Secretary for about four years following 1895, and Dr. Perin was Financial Secretary in 1899–1901 to raise the Twentieth Century Fund. The office of Field Secretary seems to be virtually the same office that these men filled under a different name.

Dr. Nash defines his office as a larger office than "Financial" Secretary. He says that he is after the money, but more after the man *with* his money. "It is my most fundamental office," says Dr. Nash, "to act as a conductor of Inspiration."

So the new Field Secretary enters the great work of increasing devotion to Christ and his Church among us, and so increasing our revenues. All these facts about government and superintendency which make up our "policy" should be most intelligently studied by every young Universalist, so that we can enter upon our plans wisely and push them with energy.

The Universalist Church of to-day is adjusting itself to an environment which is entirely changed from that in which it was born, and in which it spent its first hundred years. That old environment was a theology as dreadful as imagination could conceive and words express. Our Church was born to fight that theology, and in that battle spent its first years. We have succeeded so well that we have created for ourselves an entirely new environment. To-day the ordinary hearer sees no difference between what is preached in the average Universalist pulpit and the pulpit of other churches.

We hardly know what to do next, and how to do it. The law is that when an environment suddenly changes, most of the old organisms which grew up in the old environment, and are shaped by it, are too hardened in the "cake of custom" to change to meet the new environment, and so perish. The Universalist Church is finding its new environment, and is in the throes of the struggle to adapt itself to the change. The work of the Universalist Church of to-day is practically the same as that of any other denomination. That work is to save the world from sin, and bring it to the feet of the Christ. We have asserted that this work would some day be entirely accomplished, when no other sect thought that it would be. Now many are agreeing with us that it will be done. We have all the same task, — to keep

on asserting that it will be done, and to do it.
Our special mission of fighting the popular theology, and asserting our own, has been changed, to some extent has passed away. We still have much need to assert our theology in the face of slowly dying error. The world wants to hear our inspiring gospel from all our pulpits every returning Sunday, but our main work to-day is to help mightily to do the thing that we have always believed would be done; viz., to save the world.

Our Church is learning how to do its share of that inspiring task better every year. Let every one of our young people believe and teach that all men must finally be saved; then let him proceed to save, as far as he can, the man beside him, the neighborhood around him, and, by losing himself in this service, the soul within him.

We have spoken of our theology as in three stages, — the John Murray or Relly stage, the Hosea Ballou stage, and the modern stage.

In its great central thought, our modern theology is that of Hosea Ballou. His great statement, so clearly worked out, that the atonement of Jesus was not to work a change in God, but a change in man, still stands.

Man is God's child; but he has forgotten it largely, has wandered far from home, is lost in many a despairing shadow. The work of Jesus is to find him in these shadows and these wanderings, and tell him, what is eternally true, that he is God's child, that his Father has not cast him off, that his Father yearns for him to come home. Jesus is the Elder Brother, come out to find the lost younger brothers and bring them home. Jesus shows them the way home, — he is the way. The Cross is the supreme cry of the soul of Jesus dying to reveal the love of God to all men, and the passion of that love that will lead all men home. This teaching of Ballou and his coadjutors is still the theology of the Universalist Church.

The notion that this salvation will be wrought for every soul at the moment of death has entirely passed, and is no part of the theology among us to-day. The Universalist theology of to-day is adjusting itself to the new scholarship. Since Hosea Ballou's day the theory of evolution has become the working theory of the world as truly as is the theory of gravitation. All our conceptions of God's ways with his world and his children are stated in terms of the new thought.

We will no longer say that God will "restore" all men to something they once had and lost, in the sense that all our fathers said it. We can find no record of anything man once had, and has lost, to which we want to be restored. We want to go forward, not back.

The science of Biblical Criticism has also arisen since the days of the Fathers. We know more about what the Bible is than they could know. The allegorical, fanciful interpretations of the past are gradually being displaced by the interpretation based on the same rules of grammar and history and reason that we apply to all other books. To-day we will not twist the writing from its plain, natural meaning, in the light of all the facts, as these facts are established by sound scholarship, even if we have to admit that a Bible writer was not a Universalist. We will not make our theory of the Book first, and then force the Book to fit our theories. We accept the results of all sound scholarship, as fast as these results are established. We rejoice to believe that these results make mightily for our glorious hope.

If God succeeds, Universalism will be the result. God will succeed. We have his word for that written indelibly in the Book and on all his creation and in the deathless instincts of every human soul.

The Universalist Church is specially fitted to do a great work in unifying all the denominations. This is true because it has a theology that in substance must be the theology around which all devout spirits will more and more gather. This is true because we occupy a middle position between two extremes, and in this middle position truth is found, and at it the world will come to rest. We are between those who on the one hand hold hard and irrational theology, and the great masses on the other hand that hold no theology at all. The only final resting-place between these extremes is at a rational, true theology. Let us give it to the world. The world sees great masses of people to-day carried off into so-called Christian Science and Dowieism and many other curious and more or less fantastic schemes. All these schemes contain truth, perhaps more truth than error. The Universalist Church more than any other is situated so that it can give free place and full expression to all that is true in all these systems, and eliminate the extreme and false in them.

The Universalist Church to-day is enlarging and perfecting its organization. The forward movement is on. All our live, progressive spirits are working and praying for it. We want to keep abreast with truth in every expression of it known to the world. We want to cast off all bigotry, all boasting that we have heard the final word of God, and be expansive and generous and liberal to every statement of truth in all God's great world. We want every Universalist to join his Church, and be a worker and a builder, and not merely so much baggage to carry.

We are glad to leaven other Churches, but we want to be a strong, living, growing Church ourselves. We want more children in our Sunday-school, more young people in our Unions, more instruction in missionary work, and more response to its calls. We want more systematic and regular giving, more faith in God, more love to man, more power that comes from the baptism with the Holy Spirit, more Christ-like living.

We believe that all the nations of the earth shall come and be saved. Let us make a united, earnest effort to make them come now.

INDEX.

Abbott, Lyman, at Boston, 62.
Adams, Clara, History of Y. P. C. U., 153.
Adams, John Coleman, Sermon on Ballou, 36; Report on Uniform procedure, 95.
Adams, Rev. John G., 12, 75.
Akashi, Rev., 122.
Apostolic Fathers, 17.
Association at Warwick, 87.
Associations, 90; value of, 98.
Atwood, Rev. I. M., at Canton, 158; as editor, 185; as General Superintendent, 201.
Austin, Rev. J. M., 75.

Balch, Rev. W. S., 13, 75.
Balfour, Rev. Walter, 71.
Ballou, Hosea, birth, 48; home life, 48, 49; biographies of, 49; theological struggles, 50; attempts to preach, 52; ordination, 53; marriage, 54; pastorates, 54; death, 55; Notes on Parables, 57; Treatise on Atonement, 57; on the Trinity, 58; in Murray's pulpit, 60; on sovereignty of God, 61; debate with Mr. Turner on future punishment, 64; on death saving sinners, 68; question of future punishment no importance, 69.

Ballou, Hosea, 2d, relation to Father Ballou, 49; History of Universalism, 12; meets theological class, 156; at Tuft's, 160; biography of, 13.
Ballou, Adin. Restorationists, 69–70.
Ballou, David, as treasurer, 113.
Barnum, P. T., at Gloucester, 117; at Tufts, 161.
Beecher, Rev. Edward, 12, 18.
Benneville, Rev. George de., 21, 37.
Bible, a Universalist book, 15.
Biblical Criticism, 208.
Billings, Rev. and Mrs., 123.
Biographies, 13.
Blackmer Home, 122.
Books on Universalism 187
Brooks, Rev. E. G., Our New Departure, 75; pleads for a convention, 93; introduces missionary boxes, 116.
Browning, Mrs., on our name, 10
Buchtel, John R., 75, 117, 163
Buchtel College, 163.

Cantwell, Rev. J. S., paper on Winchester profession, 105; as editor, 184.
Capen, Rev. E. H., a creed, 109; at Tufts, 160.
Canton Theological School, 157.

Cate, Rev. W., 120.
Centennial at Winchester, 106.
Centenary year, 116.
Channing and Stuart debate, 72.
Chapin, Rev. E. H., pastor in Boston, 83; in New York, 84.
Chapin, Rev. J. H., in Japan, 119; at Canton, 162.
Chicago Covenant, 200.
Children's Sunday, 136.
Church, importance of, 81.
Church, Rev. A. B., at Buchtel.
Church Harmonies, 193.
Clark, Rev. F. E., and Y. P. S. C. E., 138.
Clement, quoted, 17.
Clinton Liberal Institute, 157.
Columbus Avenue Church, 83.
Cole, Mr. E. H., at St. Lawrence, 161; in S. S. work, 132.
Committees, on organization, 93; to revise, 94; on relation of State conventions to the General, 95; on Fellowship, 96; on Foreign Missions, 119.
Commissions on Sunday-schools, 132.
Cone, Rev. O., at Canton, 161; Buchtel, 163; books of, 187.
Congregational in government, 86.
Constitution of General Convention, 94; changes in, 94
Convention of 1803, 104.
Creeds, 102, 104.

Dean, Oliver, 75, 161.
Dean Academy, 165.
Death does not save sinners, 68.
Dodge, Nehemiah, poem of, 188.
Dodge, Rev. J. S., book of, 187.

Eastern Association, 90.
Eddy, Rev. Richard, History of Universalism, 12; five sources of U., 21.
Emerson, Rev. G. H., 75, 183.

Factors, four of denomination, 77.
Father's Work, 16.
Fifty Notable Years, 12.
Financial Secretaries, 203.
Fisher, Ebenezer, 75; President at Canton, 158.
Field Secretaries, 203.
Five points of theology, 108.
Funds of Convention, 113, 115.
Future punishment stated, 66.
Foreign Missions, 118.

Gaines, Rev. A. G., at Canton, 161.
General Convention, formation of, 95; constitution of, 94; composition of, 97; officers of, 97; biennial sessions of, 98; funds of, 199.
Goddard, Thomas and Mary, 75; at Tufts, 161.
Goddard Seminary, 165.
Good Luck, 26.
Good Will Songs, 197.
Gloria Patri, 192; revised, 194.
Gloucester, 29, 79, 117.
Grosh, Rev. A. B., 75.
Gunnison, Rev. A., 132; at Canton, 158.

Hanson, Rev. J. W., in Scotland, 176; Manna, 190; books of, 19.
Harsen, Jacob, 157.
Hart, Mr. W. H., Superintendent's Bureau, 128.

Helper, S. S., 127, 179.
Home Missions, 123.
Hymn Books, 194–196.

Imai, Miss Tame, 122, 176.
Ito, Rev. S., 122.

Japan Mission, 118.
Japan Ministers, 122.
Joy, John D. W., 76; at Tufts, 161.

Keirn, Rev. G. I., in Japan, 121.
Kendall, Rev. Paul, at Lombard, 162.

Lathe, Rev. Z., on creed, 105.
Lee, Rev. J. S., trains ministers, 156; at Canton, 161.
Lee, Rev. J. C., at Canton, 162.
Leonard, Rev. C. H., Children's Sunday, 135; Book of Prayer, 192; Tufts, 158.
Leavitt, Rev. Edgar, in Japan, 120.
Liturgies, 192.
Lombard, Benjamin, 75.
Lombard College, 159, 162.

Manna, 190.
Manuals, latest for S.S.'s, 131, 190.
Marsh, Mrs. G. B., 139.
Metcalf, Hon. H. B., 84; at Tufts, 160.
Miner, Rev. A. A., at Columbus Avenue, 83; at Tufts, 160.
Mission Circles, 175, 177.
Missionary Boxes, 116; funds, 113.
Mitchell, Rev., last of the Rellyans, 46.

Murray, Rev. John early life, 24; sails for America, 25; meets Potter, 25; first sermon in America, 26; itineracy, 28; attacked, 29; goes to Gloucester, 30; marries, 29; death, 32; lawsuits, 31; desires closer association, 87; children, 133; charged with concealment, 45; theology of, 41–45.
Murray, Mrs. Judith, 29, 60.
Murray Grove Association, 26.
Murray Centenary, 115.
Murray, Noah, on Creed, 105.

Nash, Rev. C. E., at Lombard, 163; Field Secretary, 203.
N. Y. Universalist Educational Society, 157.
Newport not assembling, 172.
Northern Association, 90.
Northwestern Association, 92.

Old Orchard Street Church, 82.
Onward, 144.
Origen, 18.
Osborn, Miss, in Japan, 121.
Oxford Association, 33, 88; parent of General Convention, 89.

Packard, Sylvanus, at Tufts, 161.
Paige, Rev. L. R., 75.
Parishes, 79
Parker, Prof., at Lombard, 162.
Pastors' wives, 167.
Perin, Rev. G. L., Japan Mission, 119, 120.
Philadelphia Convention, created, 88; creed of, 102; on future punishment, 66; on uniform service, 191.

Potter, Thomas, 25.
Priest, Rev. Ira, at Buchtel, 163.
Principles, five, 108.
Publishing House, 11, 180.

Quinby, Rev. G. W., 186.
Quinby, Mrs., 173.

Register, 12.
Relly's Union, 23.
Rellyans, 29, 42, 79.
Rellyanism, 43–45.
Restorationists, 69–70.
Rexford, Rev. E. L. at Buchtel, 163.
Rice, Rev. Clarence, in Japan, 120.
Rich, Rev. Caleb, 34, 45, 66.
Ropes at Canton, 157.
Rugg, Rev. H. W., 119; secretary, 204.
Rush, Benjamin, M.D., 101, 125.
Ryder, Rev. W. H., on our name, 10; at Canton, 162; at Tufts, 160; at Lombard, 163; at St. Paul's Church, 84.

Safford, Rev. O. F., Life of Ballou, 49; on Helper, 127.
Sawyer, Rev. T. J., 13, 46; educational work, 155; Orchard St., 156; Tufts, 160.
Sawyer, Mrs. Caroline, 13, 169.
Saxe, Rev. Asa Field, secretary, 116.
Schouler, Miss, 120.
Schrock, Miss, 121.
Scotland Mission, 176.
Shinn, Rev. Q. H., 203.
Siegfolk's book, 22.
Smith, Rev. S. B., trains ministers, 156.

Societies, 79, 80.
Soule, Mrs., 169, 172.
Southern Association, 90.
Stacy, Rev. N., at Winchester 105; baptism of a child by, 134 opposes theological schools 155.
St. Lawrence University, 161.
State Conventions, 199.
State Conferences, 199.
Streeter, Rev. Adam, 35.
Summer Meetings, 99.
Sunday Schools, early, 126; catechisms for, 126; Helper, 127 Commission on, 128, 129; departments of, 130; Superintendents of, 132; Service book for, 190; new manuals for 190
Superintendency, 201–202.

Taxation of Universalists, 31 101.
Thayer, Rev. T. B., 75, 118.
Theodore, 18.
Theological Schools, six early 18; modern, 157, 159, 158.
Thomas, Rev. A. C., 12, 192.
Thomas, Mrs. M. Louise, 173.
Tomlinson, Rev. D. C., canvasses N. Y., 114.
Tufts, 158, 160.
Tuttle, Rev. J. H., 83; at Minneapolis, 84.
Turner, Rev. Edward, debate with Mr. Ballou, 64.
Twentieth Century Fund, 124.

Uniform Service, 193.
Universalist, distinctive idea of 9; name, 10; favor congrega

tional government, 86; missions, 112, periodicals, 179; Magazine, 181; Herald, 185; books, 187; fitted to do a needed work, 208; "Leader," 182; statistics of, 199.

Universalism condemned, 19; in America before Murray, 21.

Westbrook Seminary, 164.
Western Association, 90.
Whittemore, Rev. Thomas, History of Universalism, 20; on Divine Sovereignty, 62; on future punishment, 69; life of, 73.
Williamson, Rev. I. D., on Divine Sovereignty, 62.
Winchester, Rev. Elhanan, 35–40. 101.

Winchester Convention, 104; confession, 104; criticisms of creed, 107; Centenary, 106.
W. C. A., The, 170–174.
W. U. M. S., The, 176.
Women Preachers, 167.
Women Workers, 168, 170.

Y. P. M. A., The, 139.
Y. P. S. C. E., The, 138, 140.
Y. P. C. U. The beginning, 142; first officers, 143; periodicals, 144; conventions of, 144; Jubilee of, 145; presidents of, 146; Officials of, 147; Mission points, 148, 149; Two cents a week, 150; funds, 150; Junior Unions, 150; Song books, 151; departments of, 152; in Memoriam. 154.

www.ingramcontent.com/pod-product-compliance
Lightning Source LLC
LaVergne TN
LVHW031629070426
835507LV00024B/3400